BHAMINIVILASA

BHAMINIVILASA

of

JAGANNATH PANDIT

(Prastavikavilasa & Shantivilasa)

Edited with a complete translation into English, Prose Order, Introduction, Notes and Appendices by

E.V. Dadape
D.G. Apte

Foreword by

B.C. Lele

MOTILAL BANARSIDASS PUBLISHERS
PRIVATE LIMITED • DELHI

Reprint : Delhi, 1994

First Published : Baroda, 1935

ISBN: 81-208-1170-4

Also available at:

MOTILAL BANARSIDASS

41 U.A. Bungalow Road, Jawahar Nagar, Delhi 110 007
120 Royapettah High Road, Mylapore, Madras 600 004
16 St. Mark's Road, Bangalore 560 001
Ashok Rajpath, Patna 800 004
Chowk, Varanasi 221 001

PRINTED IN INDIA

BY JAINENDRA PRAKASH JAIN AT SHRI JAINENDRA PRESS,
A-45 NARAINA, PHASE I, NEW DELHI 110 028
AND PUBLISHED BY NARENDRA PRAKASH JAIN FOR
MOTILAL BANARSIDASS PUBLISHERS PVT. LTD.,
BUNGALOW ROAD, DELHI 110 007

FOREWORD.

It gives me great pleasure to write a foreword to this edition of Bhaminivilasa prepared by my friends, Messrs. Dadape and Apte. To the ordinary student of Sanskrit, the name of Pandit Jagannath is familiar on account of his popular works, Gangalahari and Bhaminivilasa. But his merit is fully appreciated only by scholars and especially by students of Alankara because his Rasagangadhara is considered to be the last word on that subject. It is a matter of gratification that this great poet is being introduced to the first year students in the College.

Messrs. Dadape and Apte are critical and careful students of sanskrit literature. Being actually engaged in the teaching profession they are fully aware of the requirements of students. I am very favourably impressed by the methodical and scholarly way in which they have interpreted the text. The introduction covers all information that is available about Jagannath and his works. I hope that the efforts of the editors in bringing out this edition will be appreciated by students for whom it is chiefly intended.

B. C. LELE,
M.A., Ph.D. (Bonn).
Asst. Commissioner of Education
Baroda State
&
Former Professor of Sanskrit
Baroda College.

BARODA.
20th February 1935

PREFACE

We feel highly pleased to place this edition of Bhaminivilasa (the portion prescribed by the University of Bombay for the F. Y. A. Examination of 1936) in the hands of the students concerned. We have herein made all possible endeavours to make the book as useful to the students as possible. Almost every important compound has been solved, ample references and parallel quotations given, and notes on grammar also have been added in some important cases. Especial care has been taken to make the book particularly useful to students who took up vernaculars as second languages at the matriculation Examination.

The plan of notes that we have followed is one based upon the correct application of the principles of psychology and for the ready grasp of students. Prose order and literal translation have been deliberately put with the text. Ample Subhashitas and other verses have been quoted with the intention of widening the knowledge of the students and to simulate self-activity on their part. Almost in all अन्योक्ति, central ideas and applications have been given to facilitate the understanding of the student world In some cases we have drawn from अच्युतराय's प्रणयप्रकाशिनी and have also discussed some important readings. The abbreviations used are mostly those in Apte's guide and Apte's dictionary. Appendices on metres and alphabetical index of verses also have been given.

The text is mainly based on the edition of the book published by Mr. L. R. Vaidya in Bombay (1887 A. D.), the appendix A also being from the same book entirely. The reason why this book has been selected is that it gives the largest number of verses.

This preface cannot be concluded unless we express our hearty thanks to Dr. B. C. Lele, M.A., Ph.D. (Bonn.), for complying with our request of writing a foreword to this book. We must also thankfully mention the names of our two young friends Messrs. S. R. Falniker and B. D. Pedgaokar as well as that of Mr. D.Y.Athavale who rendered invaluable help to us in preparing the press copy and in other matters. We hope this attempt of ours will be heartily liked by the students.

June 1935

E. V. Dadape
D. G. Apte.

CONTENTS.

INTRODUCTION

Jagannatha Pandit is unanimously considered as one of the most glorious stars in the galaxy of Sanskrit poets and as such has been receiving that incredibly high degree of honour and commendation which no poet perhaps has ever been able to command at the hands of the cultured public, since the comparatively darker ages when कालिदास & भवभूति-both invaluable crest-jewels of the goddess Saraswati-are recorded to have flourished. However, one will be struck to observe that this great edifice of the unrivalled glory of our poet rests on a foundation immensely different from that of his two great predecessors and compeers in his renown. कालिदास & भवभूति built their unparalleled glory on the unprecedented poetic imageries and fascinating diction which appear in dramas like शाकुन्तल & उत्तररामचरित, and in works like रघुवंश and कुमारसम्भव. जगन्नाथ, however, had no such big work which was mainly instrumental in establishing his fame. It is a pleasant mystery that although more popular of his works such as भामिनीविलास, गंगालहरी &c. are inaccessible to an ordinary scholar, his real fame rests on them. We think, this is due to his masterly command over language and highclass polemics, linked with profound knowledge of the subject in hand, which effectively appeal to the learned scholars. In this respect our poet can be very favourably compared with the greaf English poet Milton who is unanimously accepted as the best and is read the least. It is hence in the fitness of things that a reader of a famous work like भामिनीविलास should be conversant with some important incidents, forming the outline of the biography of this "sovereign of poets".

पंडित जगन्नाथराय was born in the year 1550 A. D. in the Village मुंगुंडा in the district वेंगिनाडी in the country of आंध्र,

His father पेरमभट्ट was one of the most learned Brahmins and had mastered almost all शास्त्रs which constituted highest learning in those days. His mother's name was लक्ष्मी, who was a very pious and devout lady. जगन्नाथ himself refers to this in verse 52 of his work प्राणाभरण in the following verse,

तैलंगान्वयमंगलालयमहालक्ष्मीदयालालितः ।
श्रीमत्पेरमभट्टसूनुरनिशं विद्वल्ललाटंतपः ॥
.........श्रीमत्पंडितराजपंडितजगन्नाथो व्यधासीदिदम् ॥

In the introduction to his work रसगंगाधर he also gives the names of the विद्यागुरुs of his father in detail as follows,

श्रीमज्ज्ञानेन्द्रभिक्षोरधिगतसकलब्रह्मविद्याप्रपञ्चः
काणादीराक्षपादीरपि गहनगिरो यो महेन्द्रादवेदीत् ॥
देवादेवाध्यगीष्ट स्मरहरनगरे शासनं जैमिनीयम्
शेषांकप्राप्तशेषामलभणितिरभूत्सर्वविद्याधरो यः ॥

As a worthy son to a worthy father, जगन्नाथ also, when a mere youth, mastered all these विद्याs from his father. This explains perhaps why he calls his father a महागुरु. He was first a गुरु because he was his father and secondly because he was also his विद्यागुरु. In his introduction to the रसगंगाधर he says पाषाणादपि पीयूषं स्यन्दते यस्य मायया । तं वन्दे पेरुभट्टाख्यं लक्ष्मीकान्तं महागुरुम् ॥ After the death of his loving mother, जगन्नाथ was married to भामिनी, who also, it is said, besides being greatly devoted to her husband, was well versed in शास्त्रs. But as ill - luck would have it, by the death of his beloved wife, जगन्नाथ was thrown into an abyss of sorrow and disgust of the world for a long time. This is perhaps imprinted in the following verse of his करुणविलास. सर्वेऽपि विस्मृतिपथं विषयाः प्रयाताः । विद्याऽपि खेदगलिता विकलीबभूव ॥ सा केवलं हरिणशावकलोचना मे । नैवापयाति हृदयादधिदेवतेव । (भा. वि. ३-३) But his grief allayed as time passed on, and he once more made up his mind to build a sound reputation and left his country forthwith.

It is said that before he started on his tour he propitiated the goddess बालात्रिपुरसुंदरी and got from her the following boon, आकुरु देशं विचरेः मा कुरु परवादिनिर्जये शंकाम् । स्वीकुरु वरमेकं मे व्याकुरु भो वत्स शास्त्राणि ॥ In the course of his travels he arrived at Jeypore and was adequately appreciated by the then ruling prince राजा भगवानदास — the brother of भानुमति, the wife of अकबर — and opened a college which in a short time, became famous because of the students of जगन्नाथ, who brought credit to his institution after prosecuting their studies in शास्त्र like न्याय, वेदान्त, व्याकरण, etc. there Thus when जगन्नाथ was leading a calm yet public life, an event happened which was to raise his reputation and make him known all over the country.

The history of India is replete with stories regarding अकबर's sincere longing for the knowledge of all religions and then of founding one common religion, based on the choicest principles of all of them, to be followed by all persons, irrespective of caste or creed. He was of course not partial towards any religion in particular, and entertained any and every learned man that came to him. Once a काजी approached him and asked him to throw a challenge to the representatives of all religions to come and discuss with him, if their religion was sufficiently systematic to withstand the tests of Islām. In a cosmopolitan spirit, this was broadcasted by the prince, and the Hindoos, who constituted the majority of his subjects found themselves in a helpless plight. They searched for a man, who should save their religion and unanimously agreed upon requesting जगन्नाथ to represent their religion which was at stake. Consequently जगन्नाथ had to shoulder the responsibility. He learnt the Persian language and studying critically the tenets of Islām he started for vanquishing his adversary.

Long and learned were the discussions which took place among the learned representatives of these two antagonistic faiths, but in the end, the काजी had to yield to the logical argument and the wide and deep knowledge of जगन्नाथ. This earned for him an almost India-wide name and fame and consequently of course made him an object of envy. After this success जगन्नाथ became an object of respect and admiration and the king would hardly feel satisfied unless he had conversed with जगन्नाथ at least for some time in a day. This friendship between the prince and the poet waxed stronger and as time passed on, he became one of those fortunate few who were basking in the sunshine of royal patronage and favour.

The king had a daughter from his Rajput wife भानुमति who had a wonderful predilection for Sanskrit learning and hence had studied the language and some scriptures under teachers, expert in that. Although born of a Mahomedan, she betrayed all signs of inclination towards and appreciation for every thing that was Hindoo and as such admired the पंडित very highly.

On one occasion when the king and the पंडित were sitting together, talking at ease, there appeared before them, the daughter of the king carrying water for her father who was sitting there and had asked her to fetch it for him. The पंडित was smitten by her bewitching beauty, and all of a sudden uttered the following picturesque verses, in which he very vividly described the paragon of beauty that was standing before him. The verses are,

इयं सुस्तनी मस्तकन्यस्तकुंभा कुसुंभारुणं चारु चेलं दधाना ।
समस्तस्य लोकस्य चेतःप्रवृत्तिं गृहीत्वा घटे न्यस्य यातीव लोकस् ॥ १ ॥

यवनी नवनीतकोमलांगी शयनीये यदि लभ्यते कदाचित् ।
अवनीतलमेव साधु मन्ये न वनी माघवनी विलासहेतुः ॥ २ ॥

यवनी रमणी विपदः शमनी कमनीयतया नवनीतसमा ।
उहिऊहि वचोऽमृतपूर्णमुखी स सुखी जगतीह यदङ्कगता ॥ ३ ॥

He was unable to overcome the passionate love for the lady and made himself bold enough to pray to the king to give her to him as a gift. He had previously known that the princess was also loving to have पंडितराज for her consort, and as the king was favourably inclined to such inter-caste marriages, he would not, in the least, object to his proposals. The verse that he instantaneously uttered runs thus, न याचे गजालिं न वा वाजिराजिं न वित्तेषु चित्तं मदीयं कथंचित् । इयं सुस्तनी मस्तकन्यस्तकुम्भा लवंगी कुरंगीदृगंगीकरोतु ॥ according to the desire of the poet and the princess, the marriage was celebrated (about the year 1605 A. D.) in all royal pomp and glory, notwithstanding the opposition of the learned orthodoxy of the town and the king gave the couple costly gifts and annual grants.

The Brahmins in Delhi felt annoyed at this undesirable event and wanted to disunite the pair and break their marriage; and to help in this pious work they sought upon the assistance of one हरदीक्षित, a learned Pandit of Benares, who also felt it a great offence given to the Hindu religion. In about 1606 i. e. immediately after the death of Akbar हरदीक्षित arrived in Delhi. A great meeting was held, in which जगन्नाथ was openly challenged for discussion about the shastric sanction for his marriage. This was a private function and the result being indecisive people gave a verdict against जगन्नाथ and he was excommunicated.

Being disgusted with constant public opposition and consequent mental and physical seclusion the Pandit started on a sojourn, and passed several years outside Delhi, in a comparatively happier mood, with his learned and loving wife, writing poems, which of course must have been highly instrumental in giving him immense relief from the persecution of his bitter enemies.

During his long absence of about two decades from Delhi, he was once invited by Jehangir, but he refused to go, seeing that the prince was vicious. However later on, in the reign of Shah Jahan, he was again invited to Delhi and a great Durbar was held to honour the पंडित and to bestow upon him, the title of पंडितराज.

Vide मूर्तिमतेव नवाबासफखानमनःप्रसादेन द्विजकुलसेवादेवाकिंवाङ्मनः-कायेन माथुरकुलसमुद्रेंदुना रायमुकुंदेनादिष्टेन सार्वभौमश्रीशहाजहान् प्रसादाधिगत-पंडितराजपदवीविराजितेन तैलंगकुलावतंसेन पंडितजगन्नाथेनासफविलासाख्ये-यमाख्यायिका निरमीयत । (आसफविलासप्रस्तावना।)

Thus when he was passing his days and had forgotten the enmity of हरदीक्षित, a shock suddenly came to him.

While one day, his wife—the Mahomedan princess—had gone out for taking a walk, she was kidnapped by some persons who were hired for the same work by हरदीक्षित, and then closed up in an old castle. For a long time the पंडित waited, but भामिनी did not return to him. He managed to send persons in search of her, but after a few days, growing impatient, he himself started, and travelled on and on in the hope of finding his beloved wife until at last he reached Benares, and resigned himself to the mercy of विश्वेश्वर, praying earnestly for his reunion with his wife, now almost lost to him.

भामिनी luckily found helpers when she was imprisoned in the castle and was successful in effecting her escape, and started to Benares where, she determined to burn herself. After some months, she—disguised as a mendicant—reached Benares. Bent upon self-immolation she was madly wandering when suddenly she came across जगन्नाथ who was also in the same plight. Thus their joy knew no bounds. Since then, the couple used to spend their time in devotion and prayer, following the rites prescribed by the shāstras. On the days of दशहरा (i. e. ज्येष्ठशुद्धप्रतिपद् to दशमी) the couple resolved upon propitiating the Ganges by a hundred repetitions of the famous पीयूषलहरी, (later known as गंगालहरी) on each of the ten days. On the very first day the incidental arrival of अप्पयदीक्षित resulted into a short conversation between these two intellectual giants. The story has been described in our notes on Bh. V. IV. 30. Thus nine days passed smoothly. On the tenth, the couple, as usual took their ablutions in the morning and began the repetitions of the गंगालहरी. After the hundred repetitions of that day were completed, he, accompanied by his यवनी wife proceeded to take a bath into the Ganges, but his enemies led by हरदीक्षित were there, who obstructed him, calling him a पतित, and hence unfit to bathe, lest the sacred water be polluted. जगन्नाथ of course was all calm He retreated and came to the top of the घाट (the steps leading to the river-water) and seating himself there began to repeat his पीयूषलहरी which constitutes fifty two stanzas. Immediately a miracle took place and the waters of the sacred river began to rise, one step for every stanza, on that घाट only, where the पंडित was sitting. When the repetition of all the fifty-two verses was completed, the पंडित became ready to throw himself into the hands of the Ganges who was beckoning to him to come to her. But the यवनी feared she would be left alone, hence on her behalf the पंडित requested to Goddess to accept यवनी also into her lap and save her. On this occasion the यवनी is said to have addressed the following verse to the Ganges:—

सुरधुनि नृपकन्ये पुण्यवंतं पुनासि । स तरति निजपुण्यैस्तत्र किं ते महत्तम् ॥
नृपवरकुलजातां यावनीं मां पुनासि । तदिह तव महत्वं, तन्महत्वं, महत्वम् ॥

Immediately the surging billows of the Ganges rose up to their heads and washed both of them away, leaving the people to wonder at the mysterious incident that had taken place before their open eyes and gaping mouths. Thus disappeared from this mortal world, the poet and scholar of immortal fame.

It must, of course, be borne in mind that the above biography is based mainly on anecdotes that are prevalent about जगन्नाथ, there being very few points which have been finally decided, and hence are not aloof from the danger of being called into question in times yet to come. However it is desirable to sound a note of caution in attaching unnece- importance to any detail and wait for some time in future when more historically authentic facts are available for reference and consequent scrutiny.

The poet's date, though he is comparatively much modern, is also a question which has not been finally settled and shares this misfortune as his worthy predecessors like Kalidasa do. Only a few sources are open for us for investigating into this matter and almost every statement has to be based more on logical inference than upon firsthand material. We have stated before that जगन्नाथ was born in

August 1550 A. D. and that he died when he was 92 years of age i.e. in 1642 A.D. If such be the case — and there seems no reason why it should be considered improbable — he can possibly have lived in the reigns of all the three emperors, Akbar, Jahangir and Shah Jahan, whose reigns collectively cover the period from 1556 A. D. to 1658 A. D. Calculating mathematically we find this easily possible. Akbar was born on the 14th of October 1542 and ascended the throne of Delhi in 1556 i.e. 6 years after the birth of Jagannatha. Supposing that जगन्नाथ was initiated when he was eight, and that he spent about a dozen years at least in acquiring the vast knowledge he possessed, we may safely infer that he was about 21 when he became Pandit. He was then married and soon after, his wife expired leaving a son behind her. It is after this that Jagannatha started on a sojourn when he was probably 24. Then he is said to have opened a college at Jaypore and his fame spread far and wide. Allowing the period of only a decade as the duration of this college, it won't be exaggerating to infer that he was about 34 when he was sufficiently wellknown to be appointed as the representative of Hinduism to take up the challenge of the Muslim Kazi for religious discussion. When he was successful he is said to have been appreciated by the King and it is said that जगन्नाथ on this occasion addressed the following verse to the emperor.

जयत्यकबरः पृथ्वीपतिरूर्जितविक्रम :
येनारातिवधूवर्गः सर्वोऽप्यकबरीकृतः ॥

At this time जगन्नाथ was about 35. This period approaches 1585 A. D. At this time Akbar was about 43 years of age and had ruled for about 29 years. Thus we find that it easily stands in the range of possibility that he was a junior contemporary of Akbar and a senior contemporary of Jahangir and Shah Jahan. Taking this into consideration all his life fits in well with the facts that have been mentioned before. Those who oppose this theory say so merely on the ground of the absence of additional positive evidence, but so long as nothing otherwise is proved, it is better to stick to what is already before us.

जगन्नाथ is a master of vigorous, effective and elegant diction and manifests conspicuously all the characteristics expected of a great poet. His wonderful imagery and unique achievements in polemics are clearly brought out in his works like the रसगंगाधर, which is the crowning work of the poet and unrivalled in its excellence. Unlike many a poet, he handles both prose and poetry with equal ease and grace which undoubtedly adds greatly to his unrivalled fame. In depicting pathos also he seems at his best. In the present verses, he sometimes appears before us as a love-sick man, sometimes as an austere philosopher, stamping all the world as a mirage and a nonentity and on other occasions as a devotee entirely dependent upon the grace of the Lord Krishna. His poems thus exhibit to an observer his majestic self playing the role of a devotee, a lover, an abstruse-thinker, grammarian, an expert controvertialist, and a versatile scholar. (For an estimate of जगन्नाथ himself about his own poetry read the following from Bh. V. III 6. निर्दूषणा गुणवती रसभावपूर्णा सालंकृतिः श्रवणकोमलवर्णराजिः। सा मामकीनकवितेव मनोऽभिरामा रामा कदापि हृदयान्मम नापयाति ॥) His scholarship also extends over various fields like that of grammar, Rhetorics, etc. and every where he has surpassed his contemporaries.

The writers on Jagannāth cannot but draw the attention of the readers to the two ignoble and yet unavoidable traits of his character, viz. his uncommon inclination towards egoism and his jealousies and trenchant attacks on his opponents. As the examples of the former we may point out a few verses at the end of the fourth Vilasa (See verses 37-38-39-40-43 & 44) Also see. " श्रुतमात्रा वाक्यार्थं करतलबदरमिव निवेदयन्ती घटना प्रसादस्य । अयं च सर्वसाधारणो गुणः । उदाहरणान्यत्र प्रायेण मदीयानि सर्वाण्येव पद्यानि (र. गं. आनन I) Also see the verse at the introduction to the र. गं. निर्माय नूतनमुदाहरणानुरूपं काव्यं मयात्र निहितं न परस्य किंचित् । किं सेव्यते सुमनसां मनसापि गन्धः कस्तूरिकाजननशक्तिभृता मृगेण ॥ All the learned persons unanimously interpret such

2

verses as insults to others of the same vocation, yet, Jagannātha deserves an indulgent treatment, since a major part of his poetry is indeed what he has described it to be. His is a "vaunting" undoubtedly, but not "vain vaunting." He is "over-confident" about his capacity, for which he should be "confident." Yet it would not be unbecoming to recommend that he should be forgiven — if at all self-praise is a very serious crime —; and should not be taken very seriously to task so as to affect his reputation as a poet and a scholar.

The second charge is that of being very trenchant and caustic in his sarcasms as manifested in नेदं रूपकम् । रूपके च बिम्बप्रतिबिम्बभावो नास्तीति केनाप्यालंकारिकंमन्येन प्रतारितस्य दीर्घश्रवस उक्तिरश्रद्धेयैव ॥ (र. गं. रूपकप्रकरण). All persons of good taste will indeed blush at this, but taking into consideration the inborn antipathy of one scholar towards another, this does not seem so condemnable as it is generally considered to be. That his writings smack of indecency in some places is a sorry fact, but can examples of a worse type of acrimony not be quoted in numbers from equally dignified writers and saints? Nay, what great person has ever spared his adversary, in his book, when once he is caught in his sure grip ? It is perhaps, taking this fact into consideration that the great कालिदास has wisely said "प्रायः समानविद्याः परस्परयशःपुरोभागाः ॥" Even great saints can not restrain themselves when they find their adversaries cornered and helpless. It is hence best to look askance at this aspect of his (Jagannātha's) works taking into consideration, the advice of the भागवत पुराण viz. "तेजीयसां न दोषाय" which frees the deliquents from all the blames resulting from their insulting words. However this is not to be imitated as the भागवत further explains, "नैतत्समाचरेज्जातु मनसाऽपि ह्यनीश्वरः विनश्यत्याचरन्मौढ्याद्यथा रुद्रोऽब्धिजं विषम् ॥
(भागवत +–३३–३०)

His views on religion are our next point of consideration. He seems to be a perfect follower of the Adwaita philosophy as propounded by Shri Shankaracharya, inasmuch as he considers कर्मन्s as subservient to ज्ञान; and as such these cannot bind a ज्ञानिन्. It is perhaps on account of this, that he refused to undergo the प्रायश्चित्तविधि for marrying a यवनी, since he was far too advanced to resort to any कर्मन् s. He many times propounds the doctrines incorporated in the books on philosophy. cf. निखिलं जगदेव नश्वरं पुनरस्मिन्नितरां कलेवरम् । अथ तस्य कृते कियानयं क्रियते हन्त जनैः परिश्रमः ॥ (Bh. V. IV. 24) So also श्वपचात्मभुवोर्निरन्तरा मम भूयात्परमात्मनि स्थितिः which is more or less parallel to शुनि चैव श्वपाके च पण्डिताः समदर्शिनः of the Bhagwat Geeta. We also recommend the students here to refer to the verse विश्वद्रीच्या भुवनमखिलं etc. (Bh. V. IV-18) and our notes thereon. This is one aspect where he is seen as a votary of the non-qualified Brahman, longing for the achievement of the identity with the eternal, according to the doctrine of the Upanishads which lays down that after the bonds of duality are cut asunder, one obtains unity and becomes free from the bonds of worldly actions. This is the ideal stage for an out-and-out Adwaitist where every thing ceases to exist and where nothing affects his mental equipoise.

As different from this comparatively dry aspect, Jaganatha is engrossed in the qualified ब्रह्म i. e. श्रीकृष्ण; (See Bh. V. IV. 17) on whom, from times immemorial eulogies have been showered like anything by his devotees. Krishna is the soother and the saviour of all his devotees and hence is popular among the learned as well as the comparatively ignorant people. जगन्नाथ sees eye to eye with the author of the Bhāgwata, inasmuch as he sees a perfect non-difference between the unqualified Brahman and the qualified कृष्ण of the Bhāgwata—किमपि ब्रह्म कृष्णाभिधानम् (Bh. V. IV. 17). He also bends before that कृष्ण, the performer of various Leelas and the consort of Gopis—cf. श्रितो वृंदारण्यं etc. (Bh. V. IV 5) and कलिंदनगनंदिनीतटसुरद्रुमालंबिनी (Bh. V. IV 3). He is merged in his solemn and sincere devotion to the son of Nanda and confidently assures his mind that, in the end Krishna will be his saviour and thus he would get salvation. cf. चेतःसरणावस्यां किं नागंता कदापि नंदसुतः ॥ (Bh. V.

IV. 28) and अस्ति मम शिरसि सततं नंदकुमारः प्रभुः परमः (Bh. V. IV 31.) (Also see our notes on the verse 3 of the 4th विलास in this connection.) When in this state of a devotee he disregards even the कर्मकाण्ड, the ज्ञानकाण्ड and other things calling them all as errors and remarks that none but the contemplation of Vishnu will save us. (Bh. V. IV. 21). Thus जगन्नाथ as a champion of भक्ति cult is the follower of रामानुज while in the matters of philosophy his verses evince the principles of शंकराचार्य's philosophy.

There is a plurality of जगन्नाथs known to history. One of them is better known to us than the other, being the poet of that name who has written the two dramas वसुमतीपरिणय and रतिमन्मथ. That the authorship of both these dramas is given to only one man, is based on the identity of some verses occurring in the two plays, and "that the same stanza is employed in both to give the name and parentage of the author." The prologues point out that he was patronized by a petty chief and that the name of his father was Balkrishna. बालकृष्णसचिवोत्तंसस्य स्वांतरम्......अस्ति न्यस्तपदोगुणैरिह जगन्नाथाभिधानः सुधीः । and that his plays were acted, in Poona, at the Ganapati festival. cf. बाजिरावप्रभुवर्यस्य नंदनेन बालाजिरायमहीसंक्रंदनेन यथा भोः कलाधर, भवता भगवतः श्रीमहागणपतेरस्मिन् महोत्सवे वार्षिके समवेता इमे रसिकाः.........विनोदयितव्या इति

वसुमतीपरिणय Act I

This points out clearly the difference between our present poet and the author of these two dramas in three main important points (1) Difference in descent (2) Difference in time, whereas one was a contemporary of Akbar, the other was a contemporary of बाळाजीबाजीराव—the third Peshwa and finally (3) Difference in place. One lived in the court of Akbar i. e. in the north whereas the other lived in the south. There are also many other जगन्नाथs mentioned as follows.

(1) जगन्नाथ—the author of a Prakrit work शशिसेना

(2) जगन्नाथ तर्कपंचानन—the author of विवादभंगार्णव who gives रुद्र as his father's name.

(3) जगन्नाथ—a resident of तैलंगण who wrote many works on politics and translated the part of the Mahābhārata dealing with politics.

(4) सम्राट् जगन्नाथ—the writer of a book on Geometry.

(5) जगन्नाथ of मिथिला—the author of अनन्तचन्द्रिकानाटक.

(6) जगन्नाथ, the son of श्रीनिवास, the author of a भाण (a kind of drama) called अनंगविजय.

(7) जगन्नाथ मिश्र—the author of सभातरंग.

(8) जगन्नाथ सरस्वती—the author of अद्वैतामृत.

(9) जगन्नाथ सूरि—the author of समुदायप्रकरण.

(10) जगन्नाथ—the author of शरभराजविलास.

(11) जगन्नाथ-the son of नारायणदैवज्ञ-the author of काव्यज्ञानविलास.

(12) जगन्नाथ—the author of अनुभोगकल्पतरु.

However none of these can be identified with our present जगन्नाथ and this suspicion need not detain us here.

Now, before giving a detailed list of the works of our author, it is more natural to give a little critical information about our present work-भामिनीविलास. The mere knowledge of the name would lead one to form a wrong idea about the book namely that the book must contain verses in which the love sports of a beautiful passionate lady are described. But the fact here is peculiar. ⟨It does not contain a continuous story like the Meghaduta, but is a mere collection of verses which the poet composed on various occasions to suit various purposes.⟩ Even in the arrangement of the verses as it stands at present there is nothing to vouchsafe the conclusion that there is a thread of meaning inwardly connecting one verse with the subsequent one. One thing, however, must be marked, namely that अच्युतराय, the author of the प्रणयप्रकाशटीका on भामिनीविलास has made vain attempts to link together the verses, but the attempt at the outset seems ridiculous and the way in which he shows the relation of the subsequent verse with the previous one, would not give the least satisfaction to any body. However one cannot help feeling astonished when one comes across the commentator's own remark in his commentary on the last (IV 32) verse which runs as under:—" एवं च मया अयं ग्रंथः काव्यप्रथनबुध्या नैव कृतः । किंतु तत्तदवसरे लीलामात्रेण तानि तानि पद्यानि कृतानि. " His opinion here is clearly expressed and yet he has not desisted from attempting to show an undercurrent of chains behind all those verses.

However this must not weigh much when we see the poet himself saying in the last verse that it is not a deliberately connected composition but that he has merely collected his verses together and sealed them up in a work. The verse runs as follows. दुर्वृत्ता जारजन्मानो हरिष्यंतीति शंकया । मदीयपद्यरत्नानां मंजूषैव कृता मया ॥ (IV 45). He clearly remarks that he was forced to do this sort of arrangement lest his verses might be plagiarized by persons who might claim them as their own productions and the name that he gave to his collection was that of his first wife who is probably the chief subject of description of his करुणविलास. Thus this is obviously a collection of miscellaneous stanzas, each stanza, complete in itself, having no context, no definite arrangement and dealing with an independent subject of its own. The work thus resembles the three शतकs of भर्तृहरी. Many of the verses have been composed to present some incidents of his own life as some say, e. g. many of his अन्योक्तिs are infused with personal touches, serving as his memoirs. The first verse, they say applies to his defeated enemies, and his almost supernatural capacities as a Pandit, the 9th verse in प्रास्ता. is said to refer to the occasion when he attempted to bring consolation to his wife यवनी who was lamenting over her low birth and so on. Almost all of these verses occur in the रसगंगाधर in one connection or another and this supports the view that has been expressed above.

Like the composition of भर्तृहरी divided into three शतकs the composition under consideration is divided into four विलासs together making one book भामिनीविलास. They are

प्रास्ताविकविलास - शृंगारविलास - करुणविलास and शान्तविलास. Some editions however read अन्योक्त्युल्लास for प्रास्ताविकविलास and शृंगारोल्लास for शृंगारविलास. The reading उल्लास instead of विलास does not stand to reason. There should be all विलासs uniformly named. Yet the substitution of अन्योक्ति (उल्लास) for प्रास्ताविक needs a more serious attention. Critically looking to the contents of this section there is nothing like प्रास्ताविक (introductory) in it. Nor does any of these sections need any introduction in view of the facts that have been proved above. The probable reason why it was termed प्रास्ताविक seems to be that these verses form the remainder, after those falling under शृंगार, करुण, and शांतरसs were taken out from the aggregate number, and were afterwards grouped into one big mass, called as:the प्रास्ताविक section and placed at the opening of the book which justifies its name but other things also must be taken into consideration, which will lead us to conclude that although the name प्रास्ताविक not altogether wrong or inappropriate, अन्योक्त्युल्लास is indeed better, since more than half the number of verses are अन्योक्तिs the rest being of the सुभाषित type. So what we would like to propose is that the first part should be named as अन्योक्ति-विलास and neither of the present two names that are printed should be given. The second and third विलासs contain verses dealing with subjects connoted by their names — the शृंगार dealing with the amorous sentiment and the करुण delineating the pathos probably dealing with his lamentation at the death of his first wife, which indeed creates an earnest feeling of sympathy for the sufferer, the last i. e. शांतविलास indeed is worthy of its name since there is serenity in almost every verse and the poet is very beautifully giving vent to his thoughts on various points, such as कर्मन्s, their utility from the point of the attainment of final bliss and his earnest longing and unfathomable faith in the fact that श्रीकृष्ण — the son of Nanda-is sure to save him in the end (See verses 21 and 31). In the closing portion of the विलास he gives free vent to his estimate of his own poetry, presenting to himself the title of पंडितराजराजितिलक (IV. 44]. He also hints at the facts that he had malicious adversaries in this field who deliberately disparaged his poems and that there were others who, though they did not express their jealousy, were reserved in showering upon his poetry the praises which it deserved on account of its extraordinary merit (see verses 40 and 41 of IV विलास). जगन्नाथ also has not borne patiently these reproaches, he has passed very trenchant remarks upon them calling them as mere dead bodies, nay, he has called them even the beasts in the human form. (See Verses 38, 39 of IV). The last verse of the Vilasa states in very clear terms his object in composing this book.

No introduction will ever be complete without giving a comprehensive list of the work of the present poet. Many of these names have been referred to by him in his work रसगंगाधर and the others are known as being his productions. The list runs as follows.

The five लहरीs to which he makes a reference in the रसगंगाधरः—मन्निर्मिताश्च पञ्चलहर्यो भावस्य. R. G. Anana I, are these (1) पीयूषलहरी (2) सुधालहरी (3) अमृतलहरी (4) करुणालहरी and (5) लक्ष्मीलहरी.

(1) पीयूषलहरी—It is entitled to appear first in the list because it is the most popular and most read and is one of the most beautiful works of Jagannātha. It consists of 52 stanzas in praise of the Ganges, thus accounting for the fact that its popular name is the गंगालहरी. All the verses are full of devotion towards the Ganges which the poet honours as his mother and his sole saviour. The beauty of this work beggars description and cannot but request the readers to enjoy it for themselves. The popular belief in connection with this work, is that this was composed, when जगन्नाथ sat on the Ghat, determined upon bringing his mundane existence to an end and immediately after this was completely sung, he disappeared in the Ganges. But this anecdote does not hold any water because many of the verses from this work have been taken up in the R. G. (See कृतक्षुद्राघौघानथ सपदि संतप्तमनसः etc. which is quoted in R. G. अनन्वयप्रकरण), which, if the case were such, would seem ridiculous. The fact is that it was composed several years before his death but he took to singing and repeating it with extra-ordinary devotion, in the ten days of the दशहरा. and ultimately was washed away- as tradition says. The metre शिखरिणी also tends to heighten the sentiment of devotion.

(२) सुधालहरी- This is an aggregate of 30 stanzas all composed with the intention of singing the glories of God Sun, on the type of the सूर्यशतक of मयूर, who is said to have been cured of leprosy by its efficacy. It is a composition which also bespeaks of the rare poetic gift of its author, the stanzas from this also are found in the R. G.

(५) अमृतलहरी- Thia is a devotional song addressed to the Jumna, consisting of only ten verses and composed on the lines of the famous नर्मदाष्टक of Shri Shankaracharya.

(४) करुणालहरी- This poem contains about sixty verses which are addressed to Vishnu—the tutelary deity of जगन्नाथ wherein he, very pathetically, beseeches him to save him from the unbearable worldly ills, which he is heir to. It is full of pathos which perhaps accounts for its name. It is also in other places titled as विष्णुलहरी but it is yet better to call it करुणालहरी, because this is the way in which the author himself has referred to it in इदं च पद्यं मयिर्मितायां भगवद्भक्तिप्रधानायां करुणालहर्यामुपनिबद्धमिति। ....

R. G. Anana I

(५) लक्ष्मीलहरी—This is a composition of about 40 verses addressed to लक्ष्मी, the consort of Vishnu. The verse 30 of this is almost the same as the verse 137 in the शृंगारविलास of the भामिनीविलास, the same verse being also quoted in रसगंगाधर.

(६) यमुनावर्णनचंपू :—This is a composition partly in verse and partly in prose (गद्यपद्यमयी वाणी चंपुरित्यभिधीयते). This is not much known to the public although it is said that it is printed in काव्यमाला. There are references from this work in the रसगंगाधर.

(7) रसगंगाधर – This is the most voluminous and the most learned of all the works on which mainly rests the reputation of our author. "It is a treatise on poetics, written in a masterly style, with great ability, sound reasoning and consummate judgment after a careful study of the previous works on the subject. Indeed it may be said that जगन्नाथ has done for poetics what भट्टोजी दीक्षित and नागोजी भट्ट after him did for grammar. In this the author discusses every disputed point at great length, fully examines the opinions of the previous writers on it and generally arrives at a satisfactory conclusion."

However one peculiar thing to be marked about this work is that it is nowhere found complete. It ends after the third quarter of the following Aryā;

किंकुर्वते दरिद्राः कासारवती धरा मनोज्ञतरा ।
कः पावनस्त्रिलोक्या........................ ॥

The natural explanation in such a case would be that the author must have died leaving the work half-done. But this argument also does not stand when we find जगन्नाथ referring to his own रसगंगाधर in one of his other works viz. चित्रमीमांसाखण्डन which opens with रसगंगाधरे चित्रमीमांसाया मयोदिता: । ये दोषास्तेऽत्र संक्षिप्य कथ्यन्ते विदुषां मुदे ॥ Thus one is forced to infer that it has been deliberatety left unfinished. Or there is a third possibility viz. the composition of these two works चित्रमीमांसाखण्डन and रसगंगाधर must have been simultaneous and these two must have been left unfinished due to the author's death. However nothing can be proposed in this connection which is free from uncertainty.

(8) मनोरमाकुचमर्दन – It is a criticizm on the book called मनोरमा which is a commentary by भट्टोजीदीक्षित on his own सिद्धान्तकौमुदी. It aims at pointing out some of the many blunders committed by भट्टोजीदीक्षित as the author i. e. जगन्नाथ himself says in the opening of the book ...गुरुद्वेषदूषितमतीनां यद्यपि पुरुदायुषेणापि न शक्यन्ते गणयितुं प्रमादास्तथापि दिङ्मात्रेण कानपि कुशाग्रीयधिषणेषु निरूपयामः । In the opening here जगन्नाथ salutes शेषवीरेश्वर who was the Guru of his father and thus this seems to be an inconsistency. However, it might possibly have been that जगन्नाथ also must have learnt some books on grammar

from his father's Guru. One of the geneological trees as given in an old book, based on the observation of मनोरमाकुचमर्दन, शब्दरत्नमंजूषा etc. mentions जगन्नाथ as the direct pupil of शेषवीरेश्वर whose father's name was शेषश्रीकृष्ण. भट्टोजीदीक्षित was the pupil of this शेषश्रीकृष्ण. वीरेश्वरगुरुं शेषं नत्वा.....the opening verse of मनोरमाकुचमर्दन shows that he was the disciple of शेषवीरेश्वर.

(9) अश्वधाटी – This is a composition of about 25 verses and is named after the metre in which it is composed. The last verse runs like this रामनाम्नः स्वपौत्रस्य कामनापूरणोत्सुकः अश्वधाटीं जगन्नाथो विश्वप्रख्यामरीचरत्। This shows that he composed it at the request of his grand son. But none of the verses has been quoted in र. गं. This has been attributed to another जगन्नाथ, the author of वसुमतीपरिणय and रतिमन्मथ, who bears the same name i. e. जगन्नाथ and yet cannot be identified with the present poet. One peculiarity, however, of this is that the 25 verses show the वृत्त्यनुप्रास of all the 25 consonants except the last II and that also with great success.

(10) प्राणाभरण–is a composition consisting of about 50 stanzas addressed to the King प्राणाभरण of Cooch Behar. It was offered to him in the year 1627 A. D. when जगन्नाथ had been there. The first verse in this work is almost identical with Bh. V. IV. 42. Almost all the other stanzas are found in the र. गं. and it may be conjectured that it was composed by culling verses from र. गं. It also bears a short commentary by जगन्नाथ himself, which in many places makes the same remarks as have been once made in the र. गं.

(11) जगदाभरण–is a composition of 50 verses addressed to one जगत्सिंह–the son of कर्णसिंह, the Rana of Udaipur. It was offered to the King in 1627. Many of the verses can be traced in र. गं. One peculiarity of this work is that many of the verses in the present poem have been taken verbatim from प्राणाभरण and the change is only in the name of the King e. g. verse 2 in this book is जाग्रतु क्षितिमण्डलोपरि जगत्सिंहो धराधीश्वरः in प्राणा. verse 2, the line is जाग्रतु क्षितिमण्डले चिरमिह श्रीकामरूपेश्वरः ॥ so also नुतो निखिलभूसुरैर्विजयते जगत्केसरी (जग. 21) is changed to नुतो निखिलभूसुरैर्जयति. कामरूपेश्वरः in प्राणा. 21. Mr. Bhāmburkar has disproved the belief that this is addressed to Dara Shukoh, Shah Jahan's eldest son; (which

is supported by Mr. Vaidya perhaps on the authority of Pandit दुर्गाप्रसाद in his edition of R. G.)

(12) आसफविलास. This work describes the exploits of one आसफखान who is identified with the नबाब आसफखान of the court of Shah Jahan. This आसफखान was later on given the title of Khān-Khānān in 1634 and he died in 1641. र. गं. mentions two verses which treat of one Asaf Khan and it might possibly be that this same आसफखान must have been referred to there. पयोधिकल्पा मतिरासफेंदोर्महीतलेऽन्यस्य न हीति मन्ये र. गं. उ. प्र.। युक्त तु याते दिवमासफेंद्रौ तदाश्रितानां यदभूद्विनाज्ञः र. ग. वि. प्र. Herein जगन्नाथ himself says that he composed this work at the instance of one रायमुकुंद of मथुरा. A part of its introduction runs as follows:—

मूर्तिमतेव नबाबासफखानमनःप्रसादेन द्विजकुलसेवाहेवांकिवाङ्मनःकायेन माथुरकुलसमुद्रेन्दुना रायमुकुंदेनादिष्टेन सार्वभौमश्रीशहाजहांप्रसादाधिगत पंडितराजपदवीविराजितेन तैलंगकुलावतंसेन पंडितजगन्नाथेन आसफाविलासाख्येयमाख्यायिका निरमीयत।

(13) भामिनीविलास - This has been treated almost in detail before. Only नागोजीभट्ट's view viz. that the book was composed with the object that it might serve as a store of illustrations, has not been mentioned before. This is easily disproved however firstly because the last verse effectively militates against it and secondly because it is more than credible that ज० could exactly foresee what verses should be composed to serve as examples in his र. गं. There is also another theory which says that the भा. वि. was composed by somebody after the death of जगन्नाथ which also may have been a fact.

(१४) चित्रमीमांसाखण्डन—This work is composed by जगन्नाथ disproving the opinions that have been expressed by अप्पयदीक्षित in his work चित्रमीमांसा, based on his own remarks made in his र. गं. on that subject e. g. in the introduction to this book he says रसगंगाधरे चित्रमीमांसाया मयोदिताः। ये दोषास्तेऽत्र संक्षिप्य कथ्यन्ते विदुषां मुदे॥

(15) पंडितराजशतक - This is also probably the work of our poet. Nothing more is however known in the matter.

अथ भामिनीविलासे

प्रास्ताविकविलासः

माधुर्यपरमसीमा सारस्वतजलधिमथनसम्भूता
पिबतामनल्पसुखदा वसुधायां मम सुधाकविता ॥ १ ॥

मम सुधाकविता वसुधायां माधुर्यपरमसीमा, सारस्वतजलधिमथनसंभूता, पिबतामनल्पसुखदा, (च) (अस्ति)।

My nectarlike poem, the utmost limit of sweetness, produced by churning the ocean of literature, is the giver of great pleasure on this earth, to those who drink (peruse) it.

दिगन्ते श्रूयंते मदमलिनगंडाः करटिनः
करिण्यः कारुण्यास्पदमसमशीलाः खलु मृगाः ।
इदानीं लोकेऽस्मिन्ननुपमशिखानां पुनरयं
नखानां पाण्डित्यं प्रकटयतु कस्मिन् मृगपतिः ॥ २ ॥

मदमलिनगण्डाः करटिनः दिगन्ते श्रूयन्ते, करिण्यः कारुण्यास्पदं, मृगाः खलु असमशीलाः इदानीं पुनः; अस्मिन् लोके अनुपमशिखानां नखानां पाण्डित्यं अयं मृगपतिः कस्मिन् प्रकटयतु ।

Elephants with their temples soiled with ichor are heard (to have fled) to the end of the quarters; the female elephants are the objects of pity; while (other) beasts of prey stand no comparison in nature. Where should then, in this world, this lord of beasts exhibit the skill of his claws, with their ends matchless (in sharpness)?

राजहंसान्योक्तिः

पुरा सरसि मानसे विकचसारसालिस्खलत्-
परागसुरभीकृते पयसि यस्य यातं वयः ।

स पल्वलजलेऽधुना मिलदनेकभेकाकुले
मरालकुलनायकः कथय रे कथं वर्तताम् ॥ ३ ॥

पुरा अस्य वयः मानसे सरसि विकचसारसालिस्खलत्परागसुरभीकृते पयसि यातं सः मराल-कुलनायकः अधुना मिलदनेकभेकाकुले पल्वलजले कथं वर्तताम् रे कथय ।

O, tell (me) how should the leader of the family of swans, who formerly passed his life in the मानस lake, in the water scented by the pollens dropping from the rows of full-blown lotuses, now remain in the water of a puddle full of multitudinous frogs, flocked together ?

विधात्रन्योक्तिः

तृष्णालोलविलोचने कलयति प्राचीं चकोरीगणे
मौनं मुञ्चति किं च कैरवकुले कामे धनुर्धुन्वति ।
माने मानवतीजनस्य सपदि प्रस्थातुकामेऽधुना
धातः किं नु विधौ विधातुमुचितो धाराधराडंबरः ॥४॥

तृष्णालोलविलोचने चकोरीगणे प्राचीं कलयति (सति), किं च कैरवकुले मौनं मुञ्चति (सति), कामे धनुर्धुन्वति (सति), अधुना मानवतीजनस्य माने सपदि प्रस्थातुकामे (सति), हे धातः, विधौ धाराधराडम्बरः विधातुं उचितः किम् ।

When the multitude of चकोरी birds, with their eyes tremulous on account of thirst, look (eagerly) towards the east, when the assemblage of night lotuses gives up its silence (i.e. blows open), when the God of love shakes his bow (of course of flowers) and when the (amorous) pride of proud ladies is about to disappear, is it then, fit for a mass of clouds. Creator ! to begin to envelope the moon ?

कमलान्योक्तिः

अयि दलदरविंद स्यन्दमानं मरन्दं
तव किमपि लिहन्तो मञ्जु गुञ्जन्तु भृङ्गाः ।

दिशि दिशि निरपेक्षस्तावकीनं विवृण्वन्
परिमलमयमन्यो बांधवो गंधवाहः ॥ ५ ॥

अयि दलदरविन्द तव स्पन्दमानं मरन्दं लिहन्तः भृङ्गाः किमपि मञ्जु गुञ्जन्तु । तावकीनं परिमलं दिशि दिशि विवृण्वन् अयं अन्यः बान्धवः गन्धवाहः।

O blooming lotus, let the bees licking your trickling honey, hum anything melodiously. (But) this other i.e. the wind diffusing your fragrance in every direction, is your disinterested friend.

कुटजान्योक्तिः

समुपागतवति दैवादवहेलां कुटज मधुकरे मा गाः ।
मकरन्दतुन्दिलानामरविन्दानामयं महामान्यः ॥ ६ ॥

हे कुटज, दैवात्समुपागतवति मधुकरे अवहेलां मा गाः । अयं (मधुकरः) मकरन्दतुन्दिलानां अरविन्दानां महामान्यः (अस्ति) ।

When the bee approaches you, by chance, O Kutaja flower, do not disrespect him. (Because) he is highly honoured by the lotuses corpulent on account of honey.

कोकिलान्योक्तिः

तावत्कोकिल विरसान् यापय दिवसान्वनान्तरे निवसन्
यावन्मिलदलिमालः कोऽपि रसालः समुल्लसति ॥ ७ ॥

(हे) कोकिल यावद् मिलदलिमालः कोऽपि रसालः समुल्लसति तावत् वनान्तरे निवसन् (त्वं) विरसान् दिवसान् यापय ।

Pass away the uninteresting days, O Cuckoo, dwelling in the heart of a forest (without cooing) until the mango tree with rows of bees flocking together, puts forth blossoms.

कमलिन्यन्योक्तिः

कमलिनि मलिनीकरोषि चेतः किमिति बकैरवहेलितानभिज्ञैः ।
परिणतमकरन्दमार्मिकास्ते जगति भवन्तु चिरायुषो मिलिन्दाः ॥ ८ ॥

(हे) कमलिनि, अनभिज्ञैः बकैः अवहेलिता इति (त्वं) चेतः किं मलिनीकरोषि । ये परिणतमकरंद मार्मिकाः मिलिन्दाः ते जगति चिरायुषो भवन्तु ।

O lotus-plant! why do you make your mind dejected because you are disrespected by the herons? May the bees, the appreciators of your fully matured honey, live long in this world.

कूपान्योक्तिः

नितरां नीचोऽस्मीति त्वं खेदं कूप मा कदापि कृथाः ।
अत्यन्तसरसहृदयो यतः परेषां गुणग्रहीतासि ॥ ९ ॥

(हे) कूप, नितरां नीचोऽस्मीति त्वं मा कदापि खेदं कृथाः । यतः (त्वं) अत्यन्तसरसहृदयः परेषां गुणग्रहीता चासि ।

O well, never give yourself up to sorrow with the thought, "I am exceedingly low (नीच)" because you have your bottom (हृदय) full of excessively sweet water (रस) and you accept (ग्रहीता) the rope (गुण) of others (in order to let the water be drawn up.)

भ्रमरान्योक्तिः

येनामन्दमरन्दे दलदरविन्दे दिनान्यनायिषत ।
कुटजे खलु तेनेहा तेने हा मधुकरेण कथम् ॥ १० ॥

येन मधुकरेण अमंदमरंदे दलदरविन्दे दिनान्यनायिषत तेन (एव मधुकरेण) हा ! कुटजे खलु ईहा कथं तेने ।

Alas! How did the bee who passed his days in a full-blown lotus, containing a great deal of honey, cherish indeed a longing for a कुटज flower?

चन्दनान्योक्तिः

अयि मलयज महिमायं कस्य गिरामस्तु विषयस्ते ।
उद्गिरतो यद्गरलं फणिनः पुष्णासि परिमलोद्गारैः ॥११॥

अयि मलयज अयं ते महिमा कस्य गिरां विषयः अस्तु, यत् (त्वं) परिमलोद्गारैः गरलम् उद्गिरतः फणिनः पुष्टिं पुष्णासि ।

O sandal, who can describe this your greatness? (lit. of whose speech can this your greatness be the subject?), since you nourish the cobras vomitting out poison, by the outpourings of your fragrance.

पाटीरान्योक्तिः

पाटीर तव पटीयान्कः परिपाटीमिमामुरीकर्तुम् ।
यत्पिंषतामपि नृणां पिष्टोऽपि तनोषि परिमलैः पुष्टिम् ॥१२॥

हे पाटीर इमां तव परिपाटीं उरीकर्तुम् कः पटीयान् यत् पिष्टः अपि त्वं पिंषतामपि नृणां परिमलैः पुष्टिं तनोषि. ।

O sandal, who is clever in imitating this your conduct, that you gratify with your fragrance even those persons who grind you, although you are ground by them.

हंसान्योक्तिः

नीरक्षीरविवेके हंसालस्यं त्वमेव तनुषे चेत् ।
विश्वस्मिन्नधुनाऽन्यः कुलव्रतं पालयिष्यति कः ॥१३॥

(हे) हंस नीरक्षीरविवेके त्वमेव आलस्यं तनुषे चेत् अधुना विश्वस्मिन् कः अन्यः कुलव्रतं पालयिष्यति ।

O swan, if you yourself become lazy in differentiating between water and milk, who else in the world, now, will observe this vow, handed down from generation to generation ?

उपरि करवालधाराकाराः क्रूरा भुजंगमपुंगवात् ।
अन्तः साक्षाद्द्राक्षादीक्षागुरवो जयन्ति केऽपि जनाः ॥१४॥

उपरि करवालधाराकाराः भुजंगमपुंगवात् क्रूराः अन्तः साक्षाद् द्राक्षादीक्षागुरवः केऽपि जनाः जयंति ।

A victory to persons of indescribable greatness whose external form is like the edge of a sword, and who are more frightful than huge snakes, but who are at heart preceptors, evidently initiating grapes in sweetness.

अरविन्दान्योक्तिः

स्वच्छन्दं दलदरविन्द ते मरन्दं
विन्दन्तो विदधतु गुञ्जितं मिलिन्दाः ।
आमोदानथ हरिदन्तराणि नेतुं
नैवान्यो जगति समीरणात्प्रवीणः ॥१५॥

हे दलदरविंद ते मरन्दं स्वच्छन्दं विंदंतः मिलिन्दाः गुंजितं विदधतु । अथ जगति आमोदान् हरिदन्तराणि नेतुं समीरणात् अन्यः नैव प्रवीणः ।

O full-blown lotus, let the bees enjoying your honey at their own pleasure make a humming sound. But in the world, none other than wind is well-versed in conveying fragrance to different quarters.

सरोन्योक्तिः

याते मय्यचिरान्निदाघमिहिरज्वालाशतैः शुष्कतां
गन्ता कं प्रति पान्थसन्ततिरसौ संतापमालाकुला ।
एवं यस्य निरन्तराधिपटलैर्नित्यं वपुः क्षीयते
धन्यं जीवनमस्य मार्गसरसो धिग्वारिधीनां जनुः ॥१६॥

"निदाघमिहिर ज्वालाशतैः अचिरात् शुष्कतां याते मयि संतापमालाकुला असौ पान्थसंततिः कं प्रति गन्ता" एवं निरंतराधिपटलैः नित्यं यस्य वपुः क्षीयते अस्य मार्गसरसः जीवनं धन्यम्, धिग् वारिधीनां जनुः ।

Blessed is the existence of this lake on the road, whose body is always growing emaciated on account of great constant mental anguish. "When I shall be soon dried up by the hundreds of rays of the summer-sun, to whom will this crowd of travellers, oppressed with excessive heat, go?" Fie upon the life of oceans.

मीनान्योक्तिः

आपेदिरेऽम्बरपथं परितः पतङ्गा
भृंगा रसालकुसुमानि समाश्रयन्ते ।
संकोचमञ्चति सरस्त्वयि दीनदीनो
मीनो नु हन्त कतमां गतिमभ्युपैतु ॥ १७॥

हे सरः त्वयि संकोचमञ्चति पतङ्गाः परितः अम्बरपथं आपेदिरे, भृङ्गाः रसालकुसुमानि समाश्रयन्ते, हन्त दीनदीनो मीनः कतमां नु गतिं अभ्युपैतु ।

O lake when you would be dried up, the birds around might have recourse to the aerial path, the bees might resort to the mango-blossoms, but alas! to what plight would the miserable fish be reduced?

कमलिन्यन्योक्तिः

मधुप इव मारुतेऽस्मिन्मा सौरभलोभमम्बुजिनि मंस्थाः ।
लोकानामेव मुदे महितोऽप्यात्माऽमुनार्थितां नीतः ॥१८॥

हे अम्बुजिनि मधुपे इव अस्मिन् मारुते सौरभलोभं मा अमंस्थाः, अमुना मारुतेन लोकानामेव मुदे महितः अपि आत्मा अर्थितां नीतः ।

O Lotus, (1) Don't consider that there is greed for fragrance in this wind like that in the bee. (2) Don't be greedy in giving your fragrance to the wind as you do when you give it to the bee; for though highly renowned, he has stooped to mendicancy for the pleasure of the people alone (i.e. his desire is not selfish).

मालत्यन्योक्तिः

गुञ्जति मञ्जु मिलिन्दे मा मालति मौनमुपयासीः ।
शिरसा वदान्यगुरवः सादरमेनं वहन्ति सुरतरवः ॥१९॥

हे मालति मिलिन्दे मञ्जु गुञ्जति मौनं मा उपयासीः । एनं वदान्यगुरवः सुरतरवः शिरसा सादरं वहन्ति ।

O मालति flower do not keep silence (i.e. do not remain closed) when the bee is melodiously humming, (because) the celestial trees, the foremost among the generous, bear him respectfully on their heads.

चन्दनान्योक्तिः

यैस्त्वं गुणगणवानपि सतां द्विजिह्वैरसेव्यतां नीतः ।
तानपि वहसि पटीरज किं कथयामस्त्वदीयमौन्नत्यम् ॥२०॥

हे पटीरज, यैः द्विजिह्वैः गुणगणवानपि त्वं सतां असेव्यतां नीतः तानपि (द्विजिह्वान्) वहसि (एतद्) त्वदीयं औन्नत्यं किं कथयामः ।

O sandal tree, what to talk of the nobility of yours, since you give resort even to those very serpents (traducers–backbiters) by whom, you, though possessed of a host of qualities, are rendered incapable of being resorted to by the good! (i.e. your nobility beggars description).

सहकारान्योक्तिः

गाहितमखिलं विश्वं परितो दृष्टाश्च विटपिनः सर्वे
सहकार न प्रपेदे मधुपेन भवत्समं जगति ॥ २१ ॥

हे सहकार मधुपेन अखिलं गहनं गाहितं. परितः सर्वे विटपिनश्च दृष्टाः (किन्तु) भवत्समं जगति न (किञ्चिदपि) प्रपेदे ।

The whole wilderness was investigated, all the trees around were observed, but, O mango tree ! the bee did not come across one like you in the world.

भ्रमरान्योक्तिः

अपनीतपरिमलान्तरकथे पदं न्यस्य देवतरुकुसुमे ।
पुष्पान्तरेऽपि गन्तुं वाञ्छसि चेद् भ्रमर धन्योऽसि ॥२२॥

हे भ्रमर अपनीतपरिमलान्तरकथे देवतरुकुसुमे पदं न्यस्य पुष्पान्तरेऽपि गन्तुं वाञ्छसि चेत्, धन्योऽसि ।

O bee, how discriminate (indiscriminate) you are, if you desire to go yet to another flower, after having stepped on (enjoyed) the flower of a celestial tree, which has removed the talk of any other fragrance. i. e. whose fragrance is unrivalled.

तटिन्यन्योक्तिः

तटिनि चिराय विचारय विन्ध्यभुवस्तव पवित्रायाः ।
शुष्यन्त्या अपि युक्तं किं खलु रथ्योदकादानम् ॥२३॥

हे तटिनि चिराय विचारयं, शुष्यन्त्या अपि विन्ध्यभुवः पवित्रायाः तव रथ्योदकादानं खलु युक्तं किम् ।

O river think for a long time (i. e. well) whether it is indeed proper for you, who are sacred because of your rise in the विन्ध्य mountain, to receive street water, even though you are dried up ?

बर्बुरान्योक्तिः

पत्रफलपुष्पलक्ष्म्या कदाप्यदृष्टं वृतं च खलु शूकैः ।
उपसर्पेम भवन्तं बर्बुर वद कस्य लोभेन ॥२४॥

हे बर्बुर पत्रफलपुष्पलक्ष्म्या कदाप्यदृष्टं, शूकैः च खलु वृतं भवन्तं वद कस्य लोभेन उपसर्पेम ।

O बर्बुर tree ! say with what attraction should we approach you, who are never seen possessed of the beauty of leaves, fruits and flowers, but are covered with thorns.

कोकिलान्योक्तिः

एकस्त्वं गहनेऽस्मिन्कोकिल न कलं कदाचिदपि कुर्याः ।
साजात्यशङ्कयाऽमी न त्वां निघ्नन्ति निर्दयाः काकाः ॥२५॥

हे कोकिल, अस्मिन् गहने त्वं एकः कदाचिदपि कलं न कुर्याः (येन) अमी निर्दयाः काकाः साजात्यशङ्कया त्वां न निघ्नन्ति ।

O cuckoo, you, while alone in the forest, should never utter sweet notes so that these merciless crows may not slay you, mistaking you to be one of their own kind.

हिमाचलान्योक्तिः

तरुकुलसुषमापहरां जनयन्तीं जगति जीवजातार्तिम् ।
केन गुणेन भवानीतात हिमानीमिमां वहसि ॥२६॥

हे भवानीतात तरुकुलसुषमापहरां, जगति जीवजातार्तिं जनयन्तीं, इमां हिमानीं केन गुणेन वहसि ?

O father of पार्वती, for what attraction, do you bear this mass of snow, which in this world, mars the beauty of the collection of trees and which inflicts pain on all living beings ?

कलभान्योक्तिः

कलभ तवान्तिकमागतमलिमेनं मा कदाप्यवज्ञासीः ।
अपि दानसुंदराणां द्विपधुर्याणामयं शिरोधार्यः ॥२७॥

हे कलभ तव अन्तिकं आगतं एतं अलिं कदापि मा अवज्ञासीः दानसुंदराणां द्विपधुर्याणां अपि अयं (अलिः) शिरोधार्यः (विद्यते) ।

O young elephant, never disregard the bee that has approached you, (for) he is to be borne on the head, even by the foremost of elephants, adorned with rut.

भ्रमरान्योक्तिः

अमरतरुकुसुमसौरभसेवनसंपूर्णसकलकामस्य
पुष्पान्तरसेवेयं भ्रमरस्य विडम्बना महती ॥२८॥

अमरतरु.....कामस्य भ्रमरस्य इयं पुष्पान्तरसेवा महती विडंबना ।

This resorting to another flower of a bee, all of whose wishes are completely fulfilled by the enjoyment of fragrance of flowers of the celestial trees, is a matter of great ridicule.

माकन्दान्योक्तिः

पृष्टाः खलु परपुष्टाः परितो दृष्टाश्च विटपिनः सर्वे ।
माकन्द न प्रपेदे मधुपेन तवोपमा जगति ॥२९॥

हे माकन्द परपुष्टाः खलु पृष्टाः परितः च सर्वे विटपिनो दृष्टाः (किंतु) मधुपेन तव उपमा जगति न प्रपेदे ।

Indeed cuckoos are inquired of, all the trees around are observed, but nothing equal to you, O mango tree, is met with by the bee.

मालाकारान्योक्तिः

तोयैरल्पैरपि करुणया भीमभानौ निदाघे
मालाकार व्यरचि भवता या तरोरस्य पुष्टिः ।
सा किं शक्या जनयितुमिह प्रावृषेण्येन वारां
धारासारानपि विकिरता विश्वतो वारिदेन ॥३०॥

हे मालाकार अस्य तरोः या पुष्टिः भवता अल्पैः अपि तोयैः भीमभानौ निदाघे करुणया व्यरचि, सा वारां धारासारानपि विश्वतः विकिरता प्रावषेण्येन वारिदेन जनयितुं शक्या किम् ?

Is it possible here for the rainy cloud, which sprinkles down all around, even heavy showers of water, to bring about that nourishment in this tree which is effected by you, O gardener, with tenderness, with even a little water in summer when the sun was scorching ?

तोयदान्योक्तिः

आरामाधिपतिर्विवेकविकलो नूनं रसा निरसा
वात्याभिः परुषीकृता दशदिशश्चण्डातपो दुःसहः ।
एवं धन्वनि चंपकस्य सकले संहारहेतावपि
त्वं सिञ्चन्नमृतेन तोयद कुतोऽप्याविष्कृतो वेधसा ॥३१॥

नूनं आरामाधिपतिः विवेकविकलः, रसा नीरसा, दशदिशः वात्याभिः परुषीकृताः, चण्डातपः दुःसहः, एवं धन्वनि चंपकस्य सकले संहारहेतौ अपि, हे तोयद, अमृतेन सिञ्चन् त्वं वेधसा कुतोऽप्याविष्कृतः ।

Indeed, the keeper of the garden is thoughtless, the earth is void of moisture, the ten quarters are rendered dusty by gusts of wind, and the scorching heat is unbearable, thus even though all these are the reasons for the destruction of the चंपक in the barren land, you, O cloud, sprinkling it with water (nectar) are manifested by Brahma, from an unexpected quarter.

हर्यन्योक्तिः

न यत्र स्थेमानं दधुरतिभयभ्रान्तनयना
गलद्दानोद्रेकभ्रमदलिकदम्बाः करटिनः ।
लुठन्मुक्ताभारे भवति परलोकं गतवतो
हरेरद्य द्वारे शिव शिव शिवानां कलकलः ॥३२॥

यत्र (द्वारे) अतिभयभ्रान्तनयनाः गलद्दानोद्रेकभ्रमदलिकदम्बाः करटिनः स्थेमानं न दधुः (तत्र) परलोकं गतवतः हरेः, (पुरा) लुठन्मुक्ताभारे द्वारे, अद्य शिव शिव ! शिवानां कलकलः भवति ।

Alas! today the female jackals are howling near the door of the dead lion, where myriads of pearls are rolling, where formerly elephants whose eyes were tremulous owing to excessive fear and around whose temples dripping with excessive ichor, the bees were hovering, did not dare to stand steadily.

बकुलान्योक्तिः

दधानः प्रेमाणं तरुषु समभावेन विपुलां
न मालाकारोऽसावकृत करुणां बालबकुले ।
अयं तु द्रागुद्यत्कुसुमनिकराणां परिमलै-
र्दिगन्तानातेने मधुपकुलझङ्कारभरितान् ॥३३॥

तरुषु समभावेन प्रेमाणं दधानः असौ मालाकारः बालबकुले विपुलां करुणां न अकृत, तु अयं (बालबकुलः) द्रागुद्यत्कुसुमनिकराणां परिमलैः दिगन्तान् मधुपकुलझङ्कारभरितानातेने ।

Loving all the trees impartially, the gardener did not show much (special) compassion towards the young बकुल plant. Still, it filled the ends of quarters with the humming of the clusters of bees with collections of flowers quickly springing from it.

वृक्षपत्यन्योक्तिः

मूलं स्थूलमतीव बन्धनदृढं शाखाः शतं मांसला
वासो दुर्गमहीधरे तरुपते कुत्रास्ति भीतिस्तव ।
एकः किन्तु मनागयं जनयति स्वान्ते ममाधिज्वरं
ज्वालालीवलयीभवन्नकरुणो दावानलो घस्मरः ॥३४॥

हे तरुपते मूलं बन्धनदृढं अतीव स्थूलं, शतं शाखाः मांसलाः, दुर्गमहीधरे वासः तत्र भीतिः कुत्रास्ति; किन्तु अयं एकः ज्वालालीवलयीभवन् अकरुणः घस्मरः दावानलः मम स्वान्ते मनाग् आधिज्वरं जनयति ।

The big trunk is firmly strengthened by roots, the many (hundred) branches are massive, your situation is on a mountain difficult to ascend, O lord of trees, whence is the danger to you ? But only the voracious relentless conflagration forming circles of the collections of flames, produces a little fever in the form of mental agony, in my mind.

मेघान्योक्तिः

ग्रीष्मे भीष्मतरैः करैर्दिनकृता दग्धोऽपि यश्चातक-
स्त्वां ध्यायन् घन वासरान्कथमपि द्राघीयसो नीतवान् ।

दैवाल्लोचनगोचरेण भवता तस्मिन्निदानीं यदि
स्वीचक्रे करकानिपातनकृपा तत्कं प्रति ब्रूमहे ॥३५॥

हे घन ग्रीष्मे भीष्मतरैः करैः दिनकृता दग्धः अपि यः चातकः त्वां ध्यायन् द्राघीयसः वासरान् कथमपि नीतवान्। इदानीं दैवात् लोचनगोचरेण भवता तस्मिन् यदि करकानिपातनकृपा स्वीचक्रे तत् कं प्रति ब्रूमहे।

O cloud, the चातक bird, though scorched with terrible rays in the summer, passed with great difficulty the long days, contemplating on you now that you who have fallen in the range of his sight through his good luck, took to kindness (cruelty) of showering hail-stones on him; with whom shall we lodge a complaint ?

जलधरान्योक्तिः

दवदहनजटालज्वालजालाहतानां
परिगलितलतानां म्लायतां भूरुहाणाम्।
अयि जलधर शैलश्रेणिशृङ्गेषु तोयं
वितरसि बहु कोऽयं श्रीमदस्तावकीनः ॥३६॥

दव...हतानां परिगलितलतानां भूरुहाणां म्लायतां सतां, अयि जलधर शैलश्रेणिशृङ्गेषु बहु तोयं वितरसि, कोऽयं तावकीन श्रीमदः ?

What sort of pride, in abundance of water, is this of yours, that you pour, O cloud, a great deal of water, on the summits of the series of mountains although the trees that are struck by the net-work of flames gathering together from the forest-conflagration, —trees, whose encircling creepers are dropped down and which consequently fade away ?

पान्थान्योक्तिः

शृण्वन् पुरः परुषगर्जितमस्य हन्त
रे पान्थ विह्वलमना न मनागपि स्याः।
विश्वार्तिवारणसमर्पितजीवनोऽयं
नाकर्णितः किमु सखे भवताम्बुवाहः ॥३७॥

रे पान्थ पुरः अस्य परुषगर्जितं श्रण्वन् हन्त मनाक् अपि विह्वलमनाः न स्याः । सखे विश्वार्तिवारणसमर्पितजीवनः अयं अबुंवाहः भवता न आकर्णितः किमु ?

O traveller, hearing the harsh thundering of the cloud before you, alas ! do not be in the least melancholy. O friend, has not this cloud, who devoted all his water (life) in allaying the distresses of the world, been heard of by you ?

चन्दनान्योक्तिः

सौरभ्यं भुवनत्रयेऽपि विदितं शैत्यं तु लोकोत्तरं
कीर्तिः किं च दिगङ्गनाङ्गणगता किन्त्वेतदेकं शृणु ।
सर्वानेव गुणानियं निगिरति श्रीखण्ड ते सुंदरा-
नुज्झन्ती खलु कोटरेषु गरलज्वालां द्विजिह्वावली ॥३८॥

सौरभ्यं भुवनत्रयेऽपि विदितं, तु शैत्यं लोकोत्तरं, किं च कीर्तिः दिगंगनांगणगता, किंन्वेतत् एकं शृणु, हे श्रीखण्ड, कोटरेषु खलु गरलज्वालां उज्झन्ती इयं द्विजिह्वावली, सर्वान् एव ते सुन्दरान् गुणान् निगिरति ।

O sandal tree, your fragrance is known even to the three worlds, extra-ordinary is your cooling power and your fame has reached the courtyard of women in the form of directions, but listen to this one thing. This row of serpents, giving out indeed flames of venom in your hollows, swallows up all your merits.

मेघान्योक्तिः

नापेक्षा न च दाक्षिण्यं न प्रीतिर्न च संगतिः ।
तथापि हरते तापं लोकानामुन्नतो घनः ॥३९॥

There is no expectation (in return), no (consciousness of) courtesy, no love (for people) nor acquaintance, yet the high—soaring cloud (the magnanimous person) removes the heat (worries) of the people.

अंबुजान्योक्तिः

समुत्पत्तिः स्वच्छे सरसि हरिहस्ते निवसति-
र्निवासः पद्मायाः सुरहृदयहारी परिमलः ।

गुणैरेतैरन्यैरपि च ललितस्यांबुज तव
द्विजोत्तंसे हंसे यदि रतिरतीवोन्नतिरियम् ॥४०॥

हे अम्बुज (तव) स्वच्छे सरसि समुत्पत्तिः, हरिहस्ते निवसतिः, (त्वं) पद्मायाः निवासः, (तव) परिमलः सुरहृदयहारी, एतैरन्यैरपि च गुणैः ललितस्य द्विजोत्तंसे हंसे यदि रतिः स्यात् (तर्हि) इयं तव अतीवोन्नतिः ।

O lotus, you are born in a pure pond, your abode is the hand of Hari, you are the residence of Laxmi, your fragrance captivates the hearts (even) of Gods, if you—who are adorned by these and other qualities–love a swan–the best of birds—it is the zenith of your greatness.

क्षीरार्णवान्योक्तिः

साकं ग्रावगणैर्लुठन्ति मणयस्तीरेऽर्कबिम्बोपमाः
नीरे नीरचरैः समं स भगवान्निद्राति नारायणः ।
एवं वीक्ष्य तवाविवेकमपि च प्रौढिं परामुन्नतेः
किं निन्दाम्यथवा स्तवानि कथय क्षीरार्णव त्वामहम् ॥४१॥

ग्रावगणैः साकं अर्कबिम्बोपमाः मणयः तीरे लुठन्ति, नीरचरैः समं प्रौढिं अपि च वीक्ष्य, हे क्षीरार्णव, त्वां अहं किं निन्दानि अथवा स्तवानि ।

On the banks, the jewels resembling the orb of the moon are rolling with the multitudes of stones; in the water is resting the भगवान् नारायण, with the aquatic animals; thus seeing, O milk—ocean, your thoughtlessness, and the zenith of your greatness, should I praise or censure you?

अर्णवान्योक्तिः

किं खलु रत्नैरेतैः किं पुनरभ्रायितेन वपुषा ते ।
सलिलमपि यन्न तावकमर्णव वदनं प्रयाति तृषितानाम् ॥४२॥

हे अर्णव एतैः रत्नैः खलु किम्, पुनः ते अभ्रायितेन वपुषा किम्, यत् तावकं सलिलं अपि तृषितानां वदनं न प्रयाति ।

O sea, indeed, what is the use of these jewels? What is the use of your body like the sky, in as much as your water does not reach the mouth of the thirsty (i. e. they cannot drink your water?)

कासारान्योक्तिः

इयत्यां संपत्तावपि च सलिलानां त्वमधुना
न तृष्णामार्तानां हरसि यदि कासार सहसा ।
निदाघे चण्डांशौ किरति परितोङ्गारनिकरं
कृशीभूतः केषामहह परिहर्तासि खलु ताम् ॥४३॥

O lake, if you do not at once quench the thirst of the thirsty (lit. distressed) even though now you have so much wealth of water, alas! whose thirst indeed will you remove, being dried up, when in summer the hot-rayed one (the sun) will diffuse around (his rays as hot as) burning charcoal?

समुद्रान्योक्तिः

अयि रोषमुरीकरोषि नो चेत्
किमपि त्वां प्रति वारिधे वदामः ।
जलदेन तवार्थिना विमुक्तान्यपि
तोयानि महान् न हा जहासि ॥४४॥

अयि वारिधे (त्वं) रोषं नो उरीकरोषि चेत् त्वां प्रति किमपि वदामः हा महान् (त्वं) तव अर्थिना जलदेन विमुक्तानि अपि तोयानि न जहासि.

O sea, we shall speak to you something if you do not get angry. Alas! you though great do not give up even those waters that have been showered by the cloud, who is your suppliant.

वर्षानद्यन्योक्तिः

न वारयामो भवतीं विशन्तीं वर्षानदि स्रोतसि जह्नुजायाः ।
न युक्तमेतत्तु पुरो यदस्यास्तरङ्गभङ्गान् प्रकटीकरोषि ॥४५॥

हे वर्षानदि जह्नुजायाः स्रोतसि विशंतीं भवतीं न वारयामः एतत्तु तव न युक्तं यदस्याः पुरः तरङ्गभङ्गान् प्रकटीकरोषि ।

O river in the rainy season, we do not prevent you from confluenting into the stream of the Ganges, but it is not proper for you that you manifest your breaking of waves, before her.

कमलान्योक्तिः

पौलोमीपतिकानने विलसतां गीर्वाणभूमीरुहां
येनाघ्रातसमुज्झितानि कुसुमान्याजघ्रिरे निर्जरैः ।
तस्मिन्नद्य मधुव्रते विधिवशान्माध्वीकमाकाङ्क्षति
त्वं चेदश्नसि लोभमम्बुज तदा किं त्वां प्रति ब्रूमहे ॥४६॥

पौलोमी...रुहां कुसुमानि येनाघ्रातसमुज्झितानि (पश्चात्) निर्जरैः आजघ्रिरे, तस्मिन् मधुव्रते अद्य विधिवशात् माध्वीकं आकाङ्क्षति (सति) (हे) अम्बुज, त्वं लोभं अश्नसि चेत् तदा त्वां प्रति किं ब्रूमहे ।

What shall we say to you, o,lotus, if you become greedy, when that bee, who first smelt the flowers of the celestial trees in the garden of Indra and which were then smelt by Gods, is through ill-luck, expecting honey from you ?

राजहंसान्योक्तिः

भुक्ता मृणालपटली भवता निपीता-
न्यम्बूनि यत्र नलिनानि निषेवितानि ।
रे राजहंस वद तस्य सरोवरस्य
कृत्येन केन भवितासि कृतोपकारः ॥४७॥

हे राजहंस यत्र भवता मृणालपटली भुक्ता, अम्बूनि निपीतानि, नलिनानि निषेवितानि, वद तस्य सरोवरस्य कृतोपकारः केन कृत्येन भवितासि ।

O king of swans, with what act will you return the obligations of that lake to you, where the clusters of lotus fibres have been enjoyed by you, waters were also drunk to your heart's content and lotuses have been tasted ?

चंचरीकान्योक्तिः

प्रारम्भे कुसुमाकरस्य परितो यस्योल्लसन्मञ्जरी-
पुञ्जे मञ्जुलगुञ्जितानि रचयंस्तानातनोरुत्सवान् ।
तस्मिन्नद्य रसालशाखिनि दशां दैवात्कृशामञ्चति
त्वं चेन्मुञ्चसि चञ्चरीक विनयं नीचस्त्वदन्योऽस्ति कः॥४८॥

हे चञ्चरीक कुसुमाकरस्य प्रारम्भे यस्य परितः उल्लसन्मञ्जरीपुञ्जे मञ्जुलगुञ्जितानि रचयन् तान् उत्सवान् आतनोः, तस्मिन् रसालशाखिनि अद्य दैवात् कृशां दशां अञ्चति सति, त्वं विनयं मुञ्चसि चेत् त्वदन्यः को नीचः ?

O bee, who is meaner than you, if you do not be modest towards that mango-tree, which is at present-through ill-luck-shorn of leaves &c, and on whose collection of blooming sprouts, you enjoyed festivals by your sweet songs, at the advent of the vernal season ?

कृष्णसारान्योक्तिः

एणीगणेषु गुरुगर्वनिमीलिताक्षः
किं कृष्णसार खलु खेलसि काननेऽस्मिन् ।
सीमामिमां कलय भिन्नकरीन्द्रकुम्भ
मुक्तामयीं हरिविहारवसुंधरायाः ॥४९॥

हे कृष्णसार, गुरुगर्वनिमीलिताक्षः अस्मिन्कानने एणीगणेषु किं खलु खेलसि ! इमां भिन्नकरीन्द्रकुम्भमुक्तामयीं हरिविहारवसुंधरायाः सीमां कलय ।

O black antelope, why do you enjoy in this forest in the herds of female antelopes, closing your eyes through great pride ? Know this to be the boundary of the play-ground of the lion, filled with pearls (dropping down) from the temples of the elephants, that have been found open.

हर्यन्योक्तिः

जठरज्वलनज्वलताऽप्यपगतशङ्कं समागतापि पुरः
करिणामरिणा हरिणा हरिणाली हन्यतां नु कथम् ॥५०॥

करिणां अरिणा हरिणा जठरज्वलनज्वलता अपि पुरा समागता अपि हरिणाली अपगतशङ्कं कथं हन्यताम् ।

How should a herd of deer, although come in front, be unscrupulously killed by a lion, who is the enemy of elephants, even though he is scorching by the gastric fire (excessive hunger).

हर्न्ययोक्तिः

येन भिन्नकरिकुंभविस्खल-
न्मौक्तिकावलिभिरञ्चिता मही ।

अद्य तेन हरिणान्तिके कथं
कथ्यतां नु हरिणा पराक्रमः ॥५१॥

येन (हरिणा) भिन्नकरिकुम्भविस्खलन्मौक्तिकावलिभिः मही अञ्चिता तेन हरिणा अद्य हरिणांतिके पराक्रमः कथं कथ्यताम् ।

How should that lion, who covered the earth with the rows of pearls dropping from the temples of elephants torn open, to-day speak about his valour to the deer ?

गजान्योक्तिः

स्थितिं नो रे दध्याः क्षणमपि मदान्धेक्षण सखे
गजश्रेणीनाथ त्वमिह जटिलायां वनभुवि ।
असौ कुम्भिभ्रान्त्या खरनखरविद्रावितमहा-
गुरुग्रावग्रामः स्वपिति गिरिगर्भे हरिपतिः ॥५२॥

हे सखे मदान्धेक्षण गजश्रेणीनाथ, इह जटिलायां वनभुवि त्वं क्षणमपि स्थितिं न दध्याः, कुम्भिभ्रान्त्या खरनखरविद्रावितमहागुरुग्रावग्रामः असौ हरपतिः गिरिगर्भे स्वपिति !

O lord of herds of elephants, whose eyes have been blinded by rut, do not tarry even a moment here in this dense forest. Here in the interior of the mountain is sleeping the best of lions, who has torn asunder with his pointed nails very big mountains (masses of rocks) mistaking them (rocks) for elephants.

गजराजपोतान्योक्तिः

गिरिगह्वरेषु गुरुगर्वगुम्फितो
गजराजपोत न कदापि संचरेः ।
यदि बुध्यते हरिशिशुः स्तनन्धयो
भविता करेणुपरिशेषिता मही ॥५३॥

हे गजराजपोत गुरुगर्वगुम्फितः (त्वं) गिरिगह्वरेषु न कदापि संचरेः । यदि स्तनंधयः हरिशिशुः बुध्यते, मही करेणुपरिशेषिता भविता ।

O cub of the lord of elephants, being elated with great haughtiness you should never stir in the caves of the mountain.

If the cub of the lion sucking his mother's breast were to be roused, only the female elephants will be left on the earth.

मालाकारान्योक्तिः

निसर्गादारामे तरुकुलसमारोपसुकृती
कृती मालाकारो बकुलमपि कुत्रापि निदधे ।
इदं को जानीते यदयमिह कोणान्तरगतो
जगज्जालं कर्ता कुसुमभरसौरभ्यभरितम् ॥५४॥

तरुकुलसमारोपसुकृती निसर्गात् कृती मालाकारः बकुलमपि आरामे कुत्रापि निदधे । इदं को जानीते यदयमिह कोणान्तरगतः जगज्जालं कुसुमभरसौरभ्यभरितं कर्ता ।

A gardener well-versed by nature, ingenious in planting the multitude of trees, planted in his garden even the बकुल tree somewhere. Who knows this that it (though) planted in some corner here will fill the whole world with the fragrance of (its) number of flowers ?

राघवान्योक्तिः

यस्मिन्वेल्लति सर्वतः परिचलत्कल्लोलकोलाहलै-
र्मन्थाद्रिभ्रमणभ्रमं हृदि हरिदन्तावलाः पेदिरे ।
सोऽयं तुङ्गतिमिंगिलाङ्गकवलीकारक्रियाकोविदः
क्रोडे क्रीडतु कस्य केलिकलहत्यक्तार्णवो राघवः ॥५५॥

यस्मिन् राघवे (तन्नामके मत्स्ये) वेल्लति (सति) सर्वतः परिचलत्कल्लोल-कोलाहलैः हरिदन्तावलाः हृदि मन्थाद्रिभ्रमणभ्रमं (आ) पेदिरे, सः अयं तुङ्गति-मिंगिलाङ्गकवलीकारक्रियाकोविदः केलिकलहत्यक्तार्णवः राघवः कस्य क्रोडे क्रीडतु ।

In whose side (lit. cavity) may this राघव fish play, (the fish) who is an expert in swallowing the bodies of the lofty तिमिंगिल fish and who quitted the sea due to the quarrel in sport, at whose movements the elephants at the quarters experience the apprehension (once experienced) at the time of the revolving of the churning mountain, because of the loud uproar of the huge waves moving all around ?

लवङ्गलतिकान्योक्तिः

लूनं मत्तगजैः कियत्कियदपि च्छिन्नं तुषारार्दितैः
शिष्टं ग्रीष्मजभीष्मभानुकिरणैर्भस्मीकृतं काननम्
एषा कोणगता मुहुः परिमलैरामोदयन्ती दिशो
हा कष्टं ललिता लवङ्गलतिका दावाग्निना दह्यते ॥५६॥

कियदपि (काननं) मत्तगजैः लूनं, कियदपि तुषारार्दितैः छिन्नम् शिष्टं (काननं) ग्रीष्मजभीष्मभानुकिरणैः भस्मीकृतं, हा कष्टं एषा कोणगता, मुहु; परिमलै दिशः आमोदयन्ती, ललिता लवङ्गलतिका दावाग्निना दह्यते. ।

Some part of the forest is (cut) destroyed by intoxicated elephants, some part is chopped by persons oppressed by frost and the rest is reduced to ashes by the terrible rays of the summer–sun Alas ! this charming clove plant (creeper) frequently rendering the directions fragrant now lying in the corner, is being burnt by the forest conflagration.

नन्दनान्योक्तिः

स्वर्लोकस्य शिखामणिः सुरतरुग्रामस्य धामाद्भुतं
पोलोमीपुरुहूतयोः परिणतिः पुण्यावलीनामसि ।
सत्यं नन्दन किं त्विदं सहृदयैर्नित्यं विधिः प्राथ्यंते
त्वत्तः खाण्डवरङ्गताण्डवनटो दूरेऽस्तु वैश्वानरः ॥५७॥

हे नन्दन, (त्वं) स्वर्लोकस्य शिखामणिः, सुरतरुग्रामस्य अद्भुतं धाम, पौलोमीपुरुहूतयोः पुण्यावलीनां परिणतिरसि (इति) सत्यम् । किन्तु सहृदयैः विधिः नित्यं इदं प्रार्थ्यते । " त्वत्तः खाण्डवरङ्गतांडवनटः वैश्वानरः दूरेऽस्तु । "

Oh Nandan garden, it is a fact that you are the crest–jewel of the heavenly world, a wonderful abode of the collection of celestial trees and the fulfilment of the series of virtuous acts of Indra and Indrani. But the Creator is being always prayed to by the merciful, thus, " Let fire, the actor, dancing on the stage in the form of the खाण्डव forest, be away from you."

कीरान्योक्तिः

स्वस्वव्यापृतिमग्नमानसतया मत्तो निवृत्ते जने

चञ्चूकोटिविपाटितारपुटो यास्याम्यहं पञ्जरात्।
एवं कीरवरे मनोरथमयं पीयूषमास्वादय-
त्यन्तः संप्रविवेश वारणकराकारः फणिग्रामणीः ॥५८॥

'स्वस्वव्यापृतिमग्नमानसतया मत्तो जने निवृत्ते चञ्चूकोटिविपाटितारपुटः अहं पञ्जराद् यास्यामि' एवं कीरवरे मनोरथमयं पीयूषं आस्वादयति अंत: वारणकराकारः फणिग्रामणीः संप्रविवेश।

"When (all) men turn away from me being engrossed in their respective occupation, I shall go away (i.e. fly off) from the cage, breaking open the pane of the door (of the cage) with the points of my beak", while thus a parrot was tasting the nectar, in the form of this desire there crept in, the best of serpents, having the shape of the trunk of an elephant.

मृगान्योक्तिः

रे चाञ्चल्यजुषो मृगाः श्रितनगाः कल्लोलमालाकुला-
मेतामम्बुधिकामिनीं व्यवसिताः सङ्गाहितुं वा कथम्।
अत्रैवोच्छलदम्बुनिर्भरमहावर्तैः समावर्तितो
यद्ग्रावेव रसातलं पुनरसौ यातो गजग्रामणीः ॥५९॥

रे चाञ्चल्यजुषः श्रितनगाः मृगाः कल्लोलमालाकुलां एतां अम्बुधिकामिनीं (*v.l.* गामिनीं) सङ्गाहितुं कथं व्यवसिताः। यद् अत्रैव उच्छलदम्बुनिर्भरमहावर्तैः समावर्तितः असौ गजग्रामणीः पुनः ग्रावा इव रसातलं यातः।

O deer, inhabiting the mountains and taking pleasure in fickleness, how have you prepared (resolved) yourself to bathe in this river which is agitated (boisterous) on account of its surging waves? since in this same (river) even that lord of elephants, has (been drowned) gone to the bottom like a stone, being once tossed by the great whirlpools of the surging mass of waters.

पोतान्योक्तिः

पिब स्तन्यं पोत त्वमिह मददन्तावलधिया
दृगन्तानाधत्से किमिति हरिदन्तेषु परुषान्।

त्रयाणां लोकानामपि हृदयतापं परिहर-
न्नयं धीरं धीरं ध्वनति नवनीलो जलधरः ॥६०॥

(हे) पोत स्तन्यं पिब, इह त्वं मददन्तावलधिया हरिदन्तेषु परुषान् दृगन्तान् किमिति आधत्से ! त्रयाणां लोकानां अपि हृदयतापं परिहरन् अयं नवनीलो जलधरः धीरं धीरं ध्वनति ।

O cub, suck milk, why do you here cast angry side glances at the ends of quarters thinking that (there are) rutting elephants(there)? This is the new and dark cloud that is sonorously thundering, (the cloud) which removes mental anguish of all three worlds even.

मेघान्योक्तिः

धीरध्वनिभिरलं ते नीरद मे मासिको गर्भः ।
उन्मदवारणबुद्ध्या मध्येजठरं समुच्छलति ॥६१॥

(हे) नीरद, अलं ते धीरध्वनिभिः मे मासिको गर्भः उन्मदवारणबुद्ध्या मध्येजठरं समुच्छलति ।

O cloud, enough of your sonorous rumblings (because) my foetus, one month old, moves about in my abdomen, considering you to be an intoxicated elephant,

सिंहान्योक्तिः

वेतण्डगण्डकण्डूतिपाण्डित्यपरिपन्थिना ।
हरिणा हरिणालीषु कथ्यतां कः पराक्रमः ॥६२॥

वेतण्डगण्डकण्डूतिपांडित्यपरिपंथिना हरिणा हरिणालीषु कः पराक्रमः कथ्यताम्।

What exploit may be related to the multitudes of the deer by the lion, who is the obstacle in the skill in the rubbing of the temples by the elephants ?

अम्भोरुहान्योक्तिः

नीरान्निर्मलतो जनिर्मधुरता वामामुखस्पर्धिनी
वासो यस्य हरेः करे परिमलो गीर्वाणचेतोहरः ।
सर्वस्वं तदहो महाकविगिरां कामस्य चाम्भोरुह
त्वं चेत्प्रीतिमुरीकरोषि मधुपे तत्त्वां किमाचक्ष्महे ॥६३॥

हे अम्भोरुह यस्य तव जनि: निर्मलत: नीरात्, यस्य (तव) मधुरता वामामुखस्पर्धिनी, यस्य तव हरे: करे वास:, परिमल: (च) गीर्वाणचेतोहर:, (त्वं) अहो महाकविगिरां कामस्य च तत् सर्वस्वं, त्वं मधुपे प्रीतिमुरीकरोषि चेत् त्वां किमाचक्ष्महे।

O lotus, you are born of clear water, your sweetness vies with the face of a beautiful lady, your habitation is the hand of Hari, your fragrance captivates the minds of Gods, you are the whole and sole possession of the words of the great poets and of cupid, yet if you entertain love for a bee, what shall we talk to you?

करिनायकान्योक्तिः

लीलामुकुलितनयनं किं सुखशयनं समातनुषे।
परिणामविषमहरिणा करिनायक वर्धते वैरम् ॥६४॥

हे करिनायक लीलामुकुलित नयनं सुखशयनं किं समातनुषे, परिणामविषमहरिणा (सह तव) वैरं वर्धते।

O lord of elephants why do you enjoy sleeping at ease with your eyes half-closed in the amorous sport? your enmity, with the lion the result of which will be grave, is waxing (thereby).

विदुषां वदनाद्वाचः सहसा यान्ति नो बहिः।
याताश्चेन्न पराञ्चन्ति द्विरदानां रदा इव ॥६५॥

विदुषां वदनाद् वाच: सहसा बहि: नो यान्ति। याता: चेत् द्विरदानां रदाइव न पराञ्चन्ति।

Words do not come out of the mouth of the wise thoughtlessly; but if once they come out they are never withdrawn like the tusks of elephants.

कल्पद्रुमान्योक्तिः

औदार्यं भुवनत्रयेऽपि विदितं संभूतिरम्भोनिधे-
र्वासो नन्दनकानने परिमलो गीर्वाणचेतोहरः।
एवं दातृगुरोर्गुणाः सुरतरोः सर्वेऽपि लोकोत्तराः
स्यादर्थिप्रवरार्थितार्पणविधावेको विवेको यदि ॥६६॥

औदार्यं भुवनत्रयेऽपि विदितं, संभूतिरंभोनिधेर्वासो नंदनकानने, परिमलो गीर्वाणचेतोहरः एवं दातृगुरोः सुरतरोः सर्वेऽपि गुणाः लोकोत्तराः (अभविष्यन्) यदि (तस्मिन्) अर्थिप्रवरार्थीतार्पणविधौ एकः विवेकः स्यात् ।

"The generosity is well known even in the three worlds; (its) birth is from the reservoir of water (sea); (its) residence is in the नन्दन garden, (its) fragrance captivates the minds of Gods," thus even all the merits of the celestial tree–the best of donors, would have been extraordinary had there been one (merit of) discretion (on his part) in the act of granting the requests of the best of supplicants.

व्याधान्योक्तिः

एको विश्वसतां हराम्यपघृणः प्राणानहं प्राणिना-
मित्येवं परिचिन्त्य मास्म मनसि व्याधानुतापं कृथाः ।
भूपानां भवनेषु किं च विमलक्षेत्रेषु गूढाशयाः
साधूनामरयो वसन्ति कति न त्वत्तुल्यकक्षाः नराः ॥६७॥

एकः अहं अपघृणः विश्वसतां प्राणिनां प्राणान् हरामि इति एवं परिचिन्त्य हे व्याध मनसि मास्म अनुतापं (अ) कृथाः । (यतः) भूपानां भवनेषु किं च विमलक्षेत्रेषु साधूनां अरयः गूढाशयाः । त्वतुल्यकक्षाः खलाः कति न वसन्ति ।

O fowler, do not feel remorse at heart after thinking thus, " I alone being relentless, destroy the life of animals confiding (in me,) " (for) there dwell in the palaces of kings and holy places thousands of wicked persons with their motives concealed, that are the enemies of the good and have a state similar to that of yours.

विश्वास्य मधुरवचनैः साधून्ये वञ्चयन्ति नम्रतमाः ।
तानपि दधासि मातः काश्यपि यातस्तवापि च विवेकः ॥६८॥

ये नम्रतमाः साधून् मधुरवचनैः विश्वास्य (तान्) वंचयन्ति तानपि (हे) मातः काश्यपि, दधासि । (हन्त) तवापि च विवेकः यातः ।

O mother earth, you bear even those who, (pretending to be) the humblest, deceive the good by inspiring them with confidence by palatable words; even you have lost discretion.

अन्या जगद्धितमयी मनसः प्रवृत्ति-
रन्यैव कापि रचना वचनावलीनाम् ।
लोकोत्तरा च कृतिराकृतिरार्यहृद्या
विद्यावतां सकलमेव गिरां दवीयः ॥६९॥

अन्या जगद्धितमयी मनसः प्रवृत्तिः, वचनावलीनां रचना काऽपि अन्या एव, लोकोत्तरा च कृतिराकृतिरार्यहृद्या विद्यावतां सकलमेव गिरां दवीयः ।

Unusual is the inclination of (their) mind, beneficial to the world; extra-ordinary is the composition of the multitude of (their) worlds; uncommon is their action; captivating is their form to the noble; (nay) everything belonging to the learned is beyond description.

कालागुर्वन्योक्तिः

आपद्गतः किल महाशयचक्रवर्ती
विस्तारयत्यकृतपूर्वमुदारभावम् ।
कालागुरुर्दहनमध्यगतः समन्ता-
ल्लोकोत्तरं परिमलं प्रकटीकरोति ॥७०॥

महाशयचक्रवर्ती किल आपद्गतः अकृतपूर्वं उदारभावं विस्तारयति । दहनमध्यगतः कालागुरुः समन्तात् लोकोत्तरं परिमलं प्रकटीकरोति ।

Tho best of the magnanimous, indeed, when fallen into adversity, extends the unprecedented generosity; sandal when cast into fire emits (all) around extraordinary fragrance.

काश्मीरजान्योक्तिः

विश्वाभिरामगुणगौरवगुम्फितानां
रोषोऽपि निर्मलधियां रमणीय एव ।
लोकंपृणैः परिमलैः परिपूरितस्य
काश्मीरजस्य कटुतापि नितान्तरम्या ॥७१॥

विश्वाभिरामगुणगौरवगुंफितानां निर्मलधियां रोषोऽपि रमणीयः एव, लोकंपृणैः परिमलैः परिपूरितस्य काश्मीरजस्य कटुताऽपि नितांतरम्या ।

Even the wrath of persons whose minds are pure, and who are filled with abundance of qualities pleasing to the whole world, is pleasing. Even the bitter taste of saffron which is filled with fragrance pleasant to the people, is excessively pleasing.

लीलालुण्ठितशारदापुरमहासंपद्भराणां पुरो
विद्यासद्मविनिर्गलत्कणमुषो वल्गन्ति चेत्पामराः ।
अद्य श्वः फणिनां शकुन्तशिशवो दन्तावलानां शशाः
सिंहानां च सुखेन मूर्धसु पदं धास्यन्ति शालावृकाः ॥७२॥

लीलालुंठितशारदाः पुरमहासंपद्भराणां पुरो विद्यासद्मविनिर्गलत्कणमुषः पामराः वल्गन्ति चेत् अद्य श्वः शकुन्तशिशवः फणिनां (मूर्धसु), शशाः दन्तावलानां मूर्धसु, शालावृकाः सिंहानां (मूर्धसु) च सुखेन पदं धास्यन्ति ।

If ignorant persons, stealing particles dropping from the house of knowledge, were to prattle before those who in a mere sport plundered the store of great wealth in the town of learning, to-day or tomorrow, (it may happen that) young birds will subdue the (hooded) serpents, the rabbits will overpower the elephants and the foxes (or dogs) will easily defeat the lions.

गीर्भिर्गुरूणां परुषाक्षराभि-
स्तिरस्कृता यान्ति नरा महत्त्वम् ।
अलब्धशाणोत्कषणा नृपाणां
न जातु मौलौ मणयो वसन्ति ॥७३॥

गुरूणां परुषाक्षराभिः गीर्भिः तिरस्कृताः नराः महत्वं यान्ति, अलब्धशाणोत्कषणाः मणयः नृपाणां मौलौ न जातु वसन्ति ।

Persons scolded by the utterances of great persons containing harsh words, attain to greatness. Never do the jewels (ornaments) (ascend) live on the heads of the kings, unless they undergo the scratching on the touch-stone.

वहति विषधरान्पटीरजन्मा
शिरसि मषीपटलं दधाति दीपः ।
विधुरपि भजतेतरां कलङ्कं
पिशुनजनं खलु बिभ्रति क्षितीन्द्राः ॥७४॥

(यत्) क्षितींद्राः खलु पिशुनजनं बिभ्रति (तत्) पटीरजन्मा विषधरान्वहति दीपः शिरसि मसी (षी) पटलं दधाति, विधुरपि कलंकं भजतेतराम् ।

(Inasmuch as) the kings nourish the wicked, the sandle-tree gives resort to the serpents, the lamp bears the coat of soot, (and) even the moon bears the stain.

सत्पूरुषः खलु हिताचरणैरमन्द-
मानन्दयत्यखिललोकमनुक्त एव ।
आराधितः कथय केन करैरुदारै-
रिन्दुर्विकासयति कैरविणीकुलानि ॥७५॥

खलु सत्पूरुषः अनुक्तः एव हिताचरणैः अखिललोकं अमन्दं आनन्दयति कथय, केन आराधितः इन्दुः उदारैः करैः कैरविणीकुलानि विकासयति ।

A good person indeed, though not requested incessantly, gives pleasure to the whole world by his charitable actions, say, at whose request does the moon cause the clusters of moon-lotuses to bloom by his benevolent rays?

कृतमपि महोपकारं पय इव पीत्वा निरान्तङ्कः ।
प्रत्युत हन्तुं यतते काकोदरसोदरः खलो जगति ॥७६॥

पय इव कृतमपि महोपकारं पीत्वा प्रत्युत निरातंकः काकोदरसोदरः खलः जगति (उपकारिणं) हन्तुं यतते ।

A wicked man, the brother of a cobra, strives, on the contrary, to kill (his benefactor) without any fear, after swallowing up (i. e. forgetting) the obligation done to him like milk (in the case of the cobra).

पाण्डित्यं परिहृत्य यस्य हि कृते बन्दित्वमालंबितं
दुष्प्रापं मनसाऽपि यो गुरुतरैः क्लेशैः पदं प्रापितः ।
रूढस्तत्र स चेन्निगीर्य सकलां पूर्वोपकारावलिं
दुष्टः प्रत्यवतिष्ठते तदधुना कस्मै किमाचक्ष्महे ॥७७॥

यस्य हि कृते पाण्डित्यं परिहृत्य (अस्माभिः) बंदित्वमालम्बितं, यो (अस्माभिः) गुरुतरैः क्लेशैः मनसा अपि दुष्प्रापं पदं प्रापितः स दुष्टः तत्र (तस्मिन् पदे)

रूढ: सकलां पूर्वोपकारावलिं निगीर्य प्रत्यवतिष्ठते चेत् तद् अधुना कस्मै किम् आचक्ष्महे ।

If that wicked person, for whom we condescended to become bards, setting aside learning; and who was raised to a position, difficult to be attained even by mind, (by us) with prodigious efforts, being established there goes against (us) after forgetting (intentionally) all the series of previous obligations, then, now what shall we say to anybody ?

खलः कापट्यदोषेण दूरेणैव विसृज्यते ।
अपायशंकिभिर्लोकैर्विषेणाशीविषो यथा ॥७८॥

अपायशङ्किभिर्लोकैः कापट्यदोषेण खलः दूरेणैव विसृज्यते, यथा आशीविषः (अपायशङ्किभिर्लोकैः) विषेण (विषदोषेण) दूरेण विसृज्यते ।

A wicked person is left at a distance by persons who apprehend danger, owing to his deceitful nature like a serpent, owing to his venom.

परार्थव्यासङ्गादुपजहदथ स्वार्थपरता-
मभेदैकत्वं यो वहति गुणभूतेषु सततम् ।
स्वभावादयस्यान्तः स्फुरति ललितोदात्तमहिमा
समर्थो यो नित्यं स जयतितरां कोऽपि पुरुषः ॥७९॥

परार्थव्यासंगात् स्वार्थपरतां उपजहदपि यः सततं गुणभूतेषु अभेदैकत्वं वहति; यस्य अन्तः ललितोदात्तमहिमा स्वभावात् स्फुरति यः नित्यं समर्थः सः कोऽपि पुरुषः जयतितराम् ।

He, who leaving aside his selfishness through (his) extreme fondness for doing good to others shows (lit. bears) great unity due to identity towards Gunas and beings, in whose mind the pleasing and generous greatness arises (lit. throbs) by his very nature and who is always capable, such a super-human person is always successful.

वंशभवो गुणवानपि सङ्गविशेषेण पूज्यते पुरुषः ।
न हि तुम्बीफलविकलो वीणादण्डः प्रयाति महिमानम् ॥८०॥

वंशभवो गुणवानपि पुरुषः सङ्गविशेषेण पूज्यते । तुम्बीफलविकलो वीणादण्डः महिमानं न हि प्रयाति ।

A man though born in a respectable family and possessed of good qualities, becomes an object of adoration by his special companionship (with the noble). A staff of a lute, though made of a good bamboo, and possessed of strings, does not attain greatness (lit. is not praised) (as long as) it is void of the frui of a gourd (i. e. void of the base made of gourd.)

अमितगुणोऽपि पदार्थो दोषेणैकेन निन्दितो भवति ।
निखिलरसायनमहितो गन्धेनोग्रेण लशुन इव ॥८१॥

(यथा) निखिलरसायनमहितः लशुनः उग्रेण गन्धेन (निन्दितो भवति) तथा अमितगुणोऽपि पदार्थः एकेन दोषेण निन्दितो भवति ।

A thing possessed of innumerable (good) qualities is condemned for (even) a single defect like garlic (लशुन) because of its violent odour, (although) prominent among all the medicines.

उपकारमेव तनुते विपद्गतः सद्गुणो नितराम् ।
मूर्छां गतो मृतो वा निदर्शनं पारदोऽत्र रसः ॥८२॥

सद्गुणः विपद्गतः मूर्छां गतः मृतः वा नितरां उपकारमेव तनुते अत्र निदर्शनं पारदो रसः ।

A meritorious man though in adversity, in swoon,or in death, confers abundant obligations, only the instance here is of the fluid mercury.

वनान्ते खेलन्ती शशकशिशुमालोक्य चकिता
भुजप्रान्तं भर्तुर्भजति भयहर्तुः सपदि या ।
अहो सेयं सीता दशवदननीता हलरदैः
परीता रक्षोभिः श्रयति विवशा कामपि दशाम् ॥८३॥

या (सीता) वनान्ते खेलन्ती शशकशिशुमालोक्य चकिता (भूत्वा) सपदि भयहर्तुः भर्तुः भुजप्रान्तं भजति, सा इयं सीता अहो दशवदननीता हलरदैः रक्षोभिः परीता, विवशा, कामपि दशां श्रयति ।

That sita, who while sporting in the skirts of the garden being startled at the sight of the young one of a hare immediately resorts to the bosom of her husband, the remover of her fears, alas !

that सीता (now) when kidnapped by रावण, and surrounded by demons, with plough-like teeth, (resorts to) is reduced to an indescribable (pitiable) condition through helplessness.

पुरो गीर्वाणानां निजभुजबलाहोपुरुषिका-
महो कारं कारं पुरभिदि शरं संमुखयतः ।
स्मरस्य स्वर्बालानयनसुममालार्चनपदं
वपुः सद्यो भालानलभसितजालास्पदमभूत् ॥८४॥

अहो ! गीर्वाणानां पुरः निजभुजबलाहोपुरुषिकां कारं कारं पुरभिदि शरं संमुखयतः स्मरस्य स्वर्बालानयनसुममालार्चनपदं वपुः सद्यो भालानलभसित-जालास्पदमभूत् ।

Alas ! the body of the God of love, who aimed his arrow towards the destroyer of (three) cities (i.e. God Shiva), after showing frequently the self-conceitedness of the strength of his arms, in front of Gods, (the body of मदन) the receptacle of worship by the garlands of flowers in the form of eyes of celestial damsels, at once became the abode of the heat of ashes of the fire (on his forehead).

The poet here refers to the verse in the कुमारसंभव 3 72 क्रोधं प्रभो संहर संहरेति यावद्गिरः खे मरुतां चरन्ति । तावत्स वह्निर्भवनेत्रजन्मा भस्मावशेषं मदनं चकार ॥

युक्तं सभायां खलु मर्कटानां
शाखास्तरूणां मृदुलासनानि ।
सुभाषितं चीत्कृतिरातिथेयी
दन्तैर्नखाग्रैश्च विपाटितानि ॥८५॥

मर्कटानां सभायां खलु (इदं) युक्तम् । तरूणां शाखाः मृदुलासनानि (स्युः), चीत्कृतिः सुभाषितं (स्यात्), दन्तैः नखाग्रैः च विपाटितानि आतिथेयी (स्यात्)

This is indeed proper in the assembly of monkeys: Twigs of trees are soft seats; their चीत्कारs are excellent speeches and their hospitality (consists of) scratches (made) by their teeth and points of their nails.

किं तीर्थं हरिपादपद्मभजनं किं रत्नमच्छा मतिः
किं शास्त्रं श्रवणेन यस्य गलति द्वैतान्धकारोत्करः ।
किं मित्रं सततोपकाररसिकं तत्त्वावबोधः सखे
कः शत्रुर्वद खेददानकुशलो दुर्वासनासञ्चयः ॥८६॥

किं तीर्थं ? हरिपादपद्मभजनं, किं रत्नम् ? अच्छा मतिः, कि शास्त्रं ? श्रवणेन यस्य गलति द्वैतांधकारोत्करः, किं सततोपकाररसिकं मित्रं ? सखे तत्वावबोधः । वद, कः खेददानकुशलः शत्रुः ? दुर्वासनासंचयः ।

What is a holy place (in this worldly existence)? Devotion to the lotus-like feet of Hari. What is a jewel ? The pure intellect. What is a science ? That on hearing which the mass of darkness in the form of dualism vanishes. What is a friend, always fond of obliging ? Knowledge of the truth. What is an enemy clever in giving pain ? The accumulation of evil desires.

निष्णातोऽपि च वेदान्ते साधुत्वं नैति दुर्जनः ।
चिरं जलनिधौ मग्नो मैनाक इव मार्दवम् ॥८७॥

चिरं जलनिधौ मग्नः मैनाकः इव मार्दवं (i. e. यथा मैनाकः मार्दवं न एति तथा) वेदान्ते (च) निष्णातोऽपि दुर्जन. साधुत्वं न एति ।

Just as the मैनाक mountain does not become soft, though plunged in ocean for a long time, so also a wicked man though well-versed in Vedanta does not attain to goodness.

नैर्गुण्यमेव साधीयो धिगस्तु गुणगौरवम् ।
शाखिनोऽन्ये विराजन्ते खण्ड्यन्ते चन्दनद्रुमाः ॥८८॥

नैर्गुण्यमेव साधीयो धिगस्तु गुणगौरवम् । अन्ये शाखिनः विराजन्ते, चन्दनद्रुमाः (तु) खण्ड्यन्ते ।

The absence of virtues (qualities) is better; fie upon the multitude of virtues. Other (ordinary) trees thrive, (while) the sandle trees are cut of.

परोपसर्पणानन्तचिन्तानलशिखाशतैः ।
अचुम्बितान्तःकरणाः साधु जीवन्ति पादपाः ॥८९॥

परोपसर्पणानन्तचिंतानलशिखाशतैः अचुम्बितान्तःकरणाः पादपाः साधु जीवन्ति.

Happily do the trees live, whose hearts are not touched by the hundreds of flames arising from fire in the form of endless anxiety which is the result of approaching others (for begging for something).

शून्येऽपि च गुणवत्तामातन्वानः स्वकीयगुणजालैः ।
विवराणि मुद्रयन्द्रागूर्णायुरिव सज्जनो जयति ॥९०॥

शून्येऽपि स्वकीयगुणजालैः गुणवत्तामातन्वानः द्राक् विवराणि मुद्रयन् च ऊर्णायुः इव सज्जनो जयति ।

A good man is successful who transforms a dunce also into a person of qualities, by means of his own stock of qualities by hiding his faults immediately like a spider who builds his web in a place which is empty, by his net of thread, and covers the openings (in the house) immediately.

खलः सज्जनकार्पासरक्षणैकहुताशनः
परदुःखाग्निशमनमारुतः केन वर्ण्यताम् ॥९१॥

सज्जनकार्पासरक्षणैकहुताशनः परदुःखाग्निशमनमारुतः खलः केन वर्ण्यताम् ।

Who can describe the wicked man who is an unique fire in burning the cotton in the form of a good man, and kind wind that aggravates the fire in the form of miseries of others.

परगुह्यगुप्तिनिपुणं गुणमयमखिलैः समीहितं नितराम् ।
ललिताम्बरमिव सज्जनमाखव इव दूषयन्ति खलाः ॥९२॥

परगुह्यगुप्तिनिपुणं गुणमयं अखिलैः नितरां समीहितं ललितांबरमिव सज्जनं खलाः आखवः इव दूषयन्ति ।

Wicked men spoil (the reputation of a) good man who is well-versed in protecting the secrets (गुह्य) of others, is possessed of good merits and is much liked by all, like mice which spoil a fine garment which is skilled in protecting the private parts (गुह्य) of others, which is full of threads and is much desired by all.

यशःसौरभ्यलशुनः शान्तिशैत्यहुताशनः ।
कारुण्यकुसुमाकाशः खलः सज्जनदुःखदः ॥९३॥

A wicked man giving pain to the good is a garlic to fragrance in the form of fame, a fire to the cold in the form of tranquillity, the sky to the flower in the form of compassion.

वृक्षान्योक्तिः

धत्ते भरं कुसुमपत्रफलावलीनां
घर्मव्यथां वहति शीतभवां रुजं च ।
यो देहमर्पयति चान्यसुखस्य हेतो-
स्तस्मै वदान्यगुरवे तरवे नमोऽस्तु ॥९४॥

यः कुसुमपत्रफलावलीनां भरं धत्ते, घर्मव्यथां शीतभवां रुजं च वहति अन्यसुखस्य च हेतोः देहमर्पयति तस्मै वदान्यगुरवे तरवे नमोऽस्तु ।

A bow to that tree, the foremost among the liberal, which bears the burden of the clusters of flowers, leaves and fruits, puts up with the afflictions of heat and cold and which sacrifices its own body for the bliss of others.

हालाहलं खलु पिपासति कौतुकेन
कालानलं परिचुचुम्बिषति प्रकामम् ।
व्यालाधिपं च यतते परिरब्धुमद्धा
यो दुर्जनं वशयितुं तनुते मनीषाम् ॥९५॥

यः दुर्जनं वशयितुं मनीषां तनुते (सः) खलु कौतुकेन हालाहलं पिपासति, कालानलं प्रकामं परिचुचुम्बिषति अद्धा च व्यालाधिपं परिरब्धुं यतते ।

He who cherishes a desire to win over a wicked man, wishes indeed to drink deadly poison with curiosity, to kiss closely the fire of final destruction or to embrace actually the lord of serpents.

जलधरान्योक्तिः

दीनानामिह परिहाय शुष्कशस्या-
न्यौदार्यं प्रकटयतो महीधरेषु ।
औन्नत्यं परममवाप्य दुर्मदस्य
ज्ञातोऽयं जलधर तावको विवेकः ॥९६॥

हे जलधर, परमगौरत्वमवाप्य इह दीनानां शुष्कशस्यानि परिहाय महीधरेषु औदार्यं प्रकटयतः दुर्मदस्य तावकः अयं विवेकः ज्ञातः।

This indiscrimination of you, O cloud, is known (to me)—you who being elated with pride on account of your exalted position, display your generosity towards the mountains, leaving aside here dried corn of the poor.

गिरयो गुरवस्तेभ्योऽप्युर्वी गुर्वी ततोऽपि जगदण्डम्।
तस्मादप्यतिगुरवः प्रलयेऽप्यचला महात्मानः ॥९७॥

Mountains are great, the earth is greater still than they, the universe is yet greater than the earth and the high-souled persons who are firm even at the world-deluge are the greatest.

व्योमनि बीजाकुरुते चित्रं निर्माति सुन्दरं पवने।
रचयति रेखाः सलिले यस्तु खले चरति सत्कारम् ॥९८॥

यः तु खले सत्कारं चरति (सः) व्योमनि बीजाकुरुते, पवने सुन्दरं चित्रं निर्माति, सलिले रेखाः रचयति।

He who treats the wicked with respect, as if sows seeds in the sky, draws a beautiful picture in wind and draws lines in water.

हारं वक्षसि केनापि दत्तमज्ञेन मर्कटः।
लेढि जिघ्रति संक्षिप्य करोत्युन्नतमासनम् ॥९९॥

केनाप्यज्ञेन दत्तं हारं मर्कटः लेढि, जिघ्रति (पश्चात्) संक्षिप्य आसनं उन्नतं करोति।

An ape, licks and smells a necklace given to him by an ignorant man and (then) raises his seat by placing that necklace below (its haunches).

मलिनेऽपि रागपूर्णां विकसितवदनामनल्पजल्पेऽपि।
त्वयि चपलेऽपि च सरसां भ्रमर कथं वा सरोजिनीं त्यजसि
॥१००॥

हे भ्रमर मलिनेऽपि त्वयि रागपूर्णां, अनल्पजल्पेऽपि (त्वयि) विकसितवदनां, चपलेऽपि (त्वयि) सरसां सरोजिनीं त्वं कथं वा त्यजसि।

O bee the lotus creeper maintains its reddish colour although you are blue (dirty), it blooms its lotuses (lit. face) although you are constantly humming (talkative), it is full of honey (full of love) even though you are volatile (and thus faithless), how do you leave it then?

स्वार्थं धनानि धनिकात्प्रतिगृह्णतो य-
दास्यं भजेन्मलिनतां किमिदं विचित्रम्।
गृह्णन्परार्थमपि वारिनिधेः पयोऽपि
मेघोऽयमेति सकलः किल कालिमानम् ॥१०१॥

यद् स्वार्थं (i. e. स्वार्थाय) धनिकात् धनानि प्रतिगृह्णतः (नरस्य) आस्यं मलिनतां भजेत् इदं किम् विचित्रं? अयं मेघः परार्थं अपि वारिनिधेः पयः अपि गृह्णन् सकलः किल कालिमानम् एति।

What wonder is there that the face of a person who takes money from the rich for selfish motives will be blackened? (why) this cloud taking even water (what to talk of wealth!) from the ocean (the store of water) even for others, indeed becomes dark all over.

जनकः सानुविशेषो जातिः काष्ठं भुजङ्गमैः सङ्गः।
स्वगुणैरेव पटीरज यातोऽसि तथापि महिमानम् ॥१०२॥

हे पटीरज, (तव) जनकः सानुविशेषः, जातिः काष्ठं, सङ्गः भुजङ्गमैः, तथापि त्वं स्वगुणैरेव महिमानं यातोऽसि।

O sandal, your father is a particular summit, by caste you are wood, your companionship is with the serpents, yet you have reached greatness only by your intrinsic merits.

कस्मै हन्त फलाय सज्जन गुणग्रामार्जने सज्जसि
स्वात्मोपस्करणाय चेन्मम वचः पथ्यं समाकर्णय।
ये भावा हृदयं हरन्ति नितरां शोभाभरैः संभृता-
स्तैरेवास्य कलेः कलेवरभुषो दैनंदिनं वर्तनम् ॥१०३॥

हे सज्जन, हन्त कस्मै फलाय गुणग्रामार्जने सज्जसि? "स्वात्मोपस्करणाय" (इति) चेत्, मम पथ्यं (wholesome) वचः समाकर्णय, ये भावा

शोभाभरैः संभृताः नितरां हृदयं हरन्ति तैरेव अस्य कलेवरपुषः कलेः दैनंदिनं वर्तनम् ।

O good man, alas! With what aim in view are you prepared to accomplish a multitude of merits? If you reply 'for decorating myself' listen to my wholesome advice. This Kali who is getting stronger gains his livelihood from those very things which, being full of great beauty, greatly attract the mind.

धूमायिता दश दिशो दलितारविन्दा
देहं दहन्ति दहना इव गन्धवाहाः ।
त्वामन्तरेण मृदुताम्रदलाम्रमञ्जु-
गुञ्जन्मधुव्रत मधो किल कोकिलस्य ॥१०४॥

O spring, having bees sweetly humming on mango-trees with tender and reddish foliage, without you, ten quarters having lotuses full-blown are turned smoky and winds (hot) like fire scorch the body of the cuckoo.

भिन्ना महागिरिशिलाः करजाग्रजाग्र-
दुद्दामशौर्यनिकरैः करटिभ्रमेण ।
दैवे पराचि करिणामरिणा तथापि
कुत्रापि नापि खलु हा पिशितस्य लेशः ॥१०५॥

करिणामरिणा करटिभ्रमेण करजाग्रजाग्रदुद्दामशौर्यनिकरैः महागिरिशिलाः भिन्नाः तथापि दैवे पराचि (सति) कुत्रापि (करिणां) पिशितस्य लेशः न खलु अपि ।

Although rocks of gigantic mountains are torn asunder by the enemy of elephants (ie. a lion) with a great deal of valour, active and prominent at the ends of nails, mistaking (the rocks) for elephants yet, fate being adverse, nowhere did he obtain even a bit of flesh (of elephants).

गर्जितामाकर्ण्य मनागङ्के मातुर्निशार्धजातोऽपि ।
हरिशिशुरुत्पतितुं द्रागङ्गान्याकुञ्च्य लीयते निभृतम् ॥१०६॥

निशार्धजातोऽपि हरिशिशुः मातुःअङ्के मनाग् गर्जितं आकर्ण्य, द्राग् उत्पतितुं निभृतं अङ्गानि आकुञ्च्य लीयते ।

Having slightly listened to the thundering while on the lap of its mother, the cub of a lion though half a night old, lurks secretly after contracting its limbs, in order to quickly pounce upon (mistaking the thunder for the voice of an elephant).

किमहं वदामि खल दिव्यमते
गुणपक्षपातमभितो भवतः ।
गुणशालिनो निखिलसाधुजनान्
यदहर्निशं न खलु विस्मरसि ॥१०७॥

हे दिव्यमते खल अभितः भवतः गुणपक्षपातं अहं किं वदामि, यत् खलु अहर्निशम् गुणशालिनः निखिलसाधुजनान् न विस्मरसि ।

O wicked person of celestial intellect, how can I (adequately) describe your partiality (enmity) for qualities, since you do not forget (i.e. remember) all the good persons possessing qualities, by day and night?

रे खल तव खलु चरितं विदुषामग्रे विविच्य वक्ष्यामि ।
अथवालं पापात्मन् कृतया कथयापि ते हतया ॥१०८॥

O wicked man, I shall relate your life (behaviour) in detail in front of the learned or O sinner, what is the use of your wretched account, even though related? (So of course I shall abstain from it).

आनन्दमृगदावाग्निः शीलशाखिमदद्विपः ।
ज्ञानदीपमहावायुरयं खलसमागमः ॥१०९॥

अयं खलसमागमः आनन्दमृगदावाग्निः, शीलशाखिमदद्विपः, ज्ञानदीप-महावायुः (च अस्ति)।

This companionship with the wicked is (like) a forest conflagration to the deer in the form of joy, a rutting elephant to the tree in the form of character and tempestuous wind to the lamp in the form of knowledge.

खलास्तु कुशलाः साधुहितप्रत्यूहकर्मणि ।
निपुणाः फणिनः प्राणानपहर्तुं निरागसाम् ॥११०॥

खलाः तु साधुहितप्रत्यूहकर्मणि कुशलाः, फणिनः निरागसाम् प्राणानपहर्तुं निपुणाः ।

The villains are experts in putting impediments in the welfare of the good. The snakes are experts in taking away the lives of innocent persons.

वदने विनिवेशिता भुजङ्गी
पिशुनानां रसनामिषेण धात्रा ।
अनया कथमन्यथावलीढा
न हि जीवन्ति जना मनागमंत्राः ॥१११॥

धात्रा रसनामिषेण पिशुनानां वदने भुजंगी विनिवेशिता अन्यथा अनया अवलीढाः जनाः अमंत्राः मनाग् (अपि) न हि जीवन्ति (इति) कथम् ।

The creator has placed a female serpent in the form of tongue, in the mouths of the wicked, otherwise how is it that persons bit by her do not live even a minute longer without the application of magic charms?

कृतं त्वयोन्नतं कृत्यमर्जितं चामलं यशः
यावज्जीवं सखे तुभ्यं दास्यामो विपुलाशिषः ॥११२॥

हे सखे त्वया उन्नतं कृत्यं कृतम् , अमलं यशः च अर्जितम् यावज्जीवं तुभ्यं विपुलाशिषः दास्यामः ।

O friend, (enemy) you have done an exalted (mean) deed and have gained untarnished fame (notoriety). So long as we live, we shall give you plenty of blessings (curses).

अविरतं परकार्यकृतां सतां
मधुरिमातिशयेन वचोऽमृतम् ।
अपि च मानसमम्बुनिधिर्यशो
विमलशारदचन्दिरचन्द्रिका ॥११३॥

The speech of persons incessantly engaged in obliging others, resembles nectar owing to its excessive sweetness, their mind is (magnanimous) like the sea and their fame resembles the moon-light of the clear autumnal moon. (i.e. gives excessive pleasure). v. l. पार्व्वणचन्द्रिका– moonlight of the full moon, because पर्व means the full moon-day.

एत्य कुसुमाकरो मे सञ्जीवयिता गिरं चिरं मग्नाम् ।
इति चिन्तयतो हृदये पिकस्य समधायि शौभिकेन शरः ।।११४।।

'कुसुमाकर एत्य मे चिरं मग्नां गिरं सञ्जीवयिता" इति चिंतयतः पिकस्य हृदये शौभिकेन शरः समधायि ।

"The spring having arrived, will restore my voice that has been silent for a long time," while a cuckoo was thus thinking, an arrow was discharged at its heart by a fowler.

निर्गुणः शोभते नैव विपुलाडम्बरोऽपि ना ।
आपातरम्यपुष्पश्रीशोभितः शाल्मलिर्यथा ।।११५।।

A man devoid of good merits does not appear to advantage, though set off by a fine (outward) display as a शाल्मलि tree though adorned with the beauty of flowers for the present moment.

पङ्कैर्विना सरो भाति सदः खलजनैर्विना ।
कटुवर्णैर्विना काव्यं मानसं विषयैर्विना ।।११६।।

A lake without mud, an assembly without wicked persons, poetry without harsh words and mind void of the sensual objects look beautiful.

तत्वं किमपि काव्यानां जानाति विरलो भुवि ।
मार्मिकः को मरन्दानामन्तरेण मधुव्रतम् ।।११७।।

काव्यानां किमपि तत्वं भुवि विरलो जानाति । मधुव्रतं अन्तरेण मरन्दानां मार्मिकः कः (विद्यते)।

In this world, scarcely any one knows the extraordinary essence of poetry; who but the bee, is the appreciator of honey (in flowers)?

सरजस्कां पाण्डुवर्णां कण्टकप्रकराङ्किताम् ।
केतकीं सेवसे हन्त कथं रोलम्ब निस्त्रपः ।।११८।।

हे रोलम्ब हन्त ! सरजस्कां पाण्डुवर्णां कंटकप्रकरांकितां केतकीं निस्त्रपः कथं सेवसे ।

O bee! How is it, alas! that you shamelessly enjoy a केतकी which is सरजस्का, पाण्डुवर्णा and कण्टकप्रकराङ्किता ?

यथा तानं विना रागो यथा मानं विना नृपः ।
यथा दानं विना हस्ती तथा ज्ञानं विना यतिः ॥११९॥

As a राग without तान, a king without respect and an elephant without rut, so is an ascetic (worthless) without knowledge (of ब्रह्मन्).

सन्तः स्वतः प्रकाशन्ते गुणा न परतो नृणाम् ।
आमोदो न हि कस्तूर्याः शपथेन विभाव्यते ॥१२०॥

नृणां सन्तः गुणाः स्वतः प्रकाशन्ते न परतः । कस्तूर्याः आमोदः शपथेन न हि विभाव्यते ।

The good merits of men shine by themselves and not from (the mouths of) others. The fragrance of musk is, indeed, not known on oath.

कस्तूर्यन्योक्तिः

अयि बत गुरु गर्वं मास्म कस्तूरि यासी-
रखिलपरिमलानां मौलिना सौरभेण ।
गिरिगहनगुहायां लीनमत्यन्तदीनं
स्वजनकममुनैव प्राणहीनं करोषि ॥१२१॥

अयि कस्तूरि, (musk) अखिलपरिमलानां मौलिना सौरभेण गर्वं मास्म बत यासीः अमुनैव सौरभेण गिरिगहनगुहायां लीनम् अत्यंतदीनं स्वजनकं प्राणहीनं करोषि ।

O musk, alas! do not pride yourself upon your fragrance which is the best of all. Owing to that (fragrance) alone you bring death to your father who is very innocent and who hides himself in the dens in the mountain-forests.

दूरीकरोति कुमतिं विमलीकरोति
चेतश्चिरन्तनमघं चुलुकीकरोति ।

भूतेषु किं च करुणां बहुलीकरोति
सङ्गः सतां किमु न मंगलमातनोति ॥१२२॥

सतां संगः कुमतिं दूरीकरोति, चेतः विमलीकरोति, चिरंतनं अघं चुलुकी-करोति, किं च भूतेषु करुणां बहुलीकरोति, किमु मंगलं न आतनोति ।

The company of the good removes ill-thoughts, purifies the mind, destroys the sin of long standing, moreover it widens humanity (the love for creatures), what auspicious thing does it not beget ?

अनवरतपरोपकारव्यग्रीभवदमलचेतसां महताम् ।
आपातकाटवानि स्फुरन्ति वचनानि भेषजानीव ॥१२३॥

अनवरतपरोपकारव्यग्रीभवदमलचेतसां महतां आपातकाटवानि वचनानि भेषजानीव स्फुरंति ।

The speech of the great, whose pure mind is always engrossed in the incessant (performance of) philanthropic deeds and which are bitter only at the beginning, shine (i. e. are) like medicines (bringing happiness in the end).

व्यागुञ्जन्मधुकरपुञ्जमञ्जुगीता-
माकर्ण्य स्तुतिमुदयन्त्रपातिरेकात् ।
आभूमीतलनतकन्धराणि मन्ये-
ऽरण्येऽस्मिन्नवनिरुहां कुटुम्बकानि ॥१२४॥

व्यागुंजन्मधुकरपुंजमंजुगीतां स्तुतिं आकर्ण्य उदयन्त्रपातिरेकात् अस्मिन्नरण्ये अवनिरुहां कुंटुबकानि आभूमीतलनतकंधराणि इति मन्ये ।

I imagine that the families (clusters) of trees in this forest have bent their necks (branches) down to the surface of the earth because of the excess of modesty (त्रप) generated in them on hearing their own praise sung by the clusters of beautifully humming bees.

मृतस्य लिप्सा कृपणस्य दित्सा
विमार्गगायाश्च रुचिः स्वकान्ते ।
सर्पस्य शान्तिः कुटिलस्य मैत्री
विधातृसृष्टौ न हि दृष्टपूर्वा ॥१२५॥

The desire to obtain, to a dead man; the desire to give, in a miserly person; the love for her own husband, in a wanton woman; calmness in a serpent; friendship in a crooked man, have never been witnessed before in the creation of God Brahman (i.e. in the world).

उत्तमानामपि स्त्रीणां विश्वासो नैव विद्यते ।
राजप्रियाः कैरविण्यो रमन्ते मधुपैः सह ॥१२६॥

उत्तमानामपि स्त्रीणां विश्वासो नैव विद्यते, राजप्रियाः कैरविण्यः मधुपैः सह रमन्ते ।

There is no faith (i.e we do not confide in) even in the best women; the night lotuses though the favourites of the moon enjoy with मधुपs (bees or drunkards).

अयाचितः सुखं दत्ते याचितश्च न यच्छति ।
सर्वस्वं चापि हरते विधिरुच्छृंखलो नृणाम् ॥१२७॥

नृणां उच्छृङ्खल: विधि: अयाचित: सुखं दत्ते याचित: च (सुखं) न यच्छति सर्वस्वं च अपि हरते ।

The unruly fate of men gives happiness when unasked and does not give it when asked (for it), (not only this but also) it takes away everthing (when it is adverse).

दोर्दण्डद्वयकुण्डलीकृतलसत्कोदण्डचण्डाशुग-
ध्वस्तोद्दण्डविपक्षमण्डलमथ त्वां वीक्ष्य मध्येरणम् ।
वल्गद्गाण्डिवमुक्तकाण्डवलयज्वालावलीताण्डव-
भ्रश्यत्खाण्डवरुष्टपाण्डवमहो को न क्षितीशः स्मरेत् ॥१२८॥

दोर्दंडद्वयकुंडलीकृतलसत्कोदंडचंडाशुगध्वस्तोद्दंडविपक्षमंडलं त्वां मध्येरणं वीक्ष्य वल्गद्गांडिवमुक्तकांडवलयज्वालावलीतांडवभ्रश्यत्खांडवरुष्टपांडवमहो क: क्षितीश: न स्मरेत् ।

Having observed in the battle field you who destroyed the circle of powerful enemies by the terrible darts (discharged) from his brilliant bow bent round by the pair of his (strong) arms, what king will not remember (i. e. every king will remember) that indignant पाण्डव (namely अर्जुन) who was standing in the खाण्डव wilderness which was destroyed by the movement of the series of flames (issuing) from the circle of arrows discharged from his twanging गाण्डिव bow ?

खण्डितानेत्रकञ्जालिमञ्जुरञ्जनपण्डिताः
मण्डिताखिलदिक्प्रान्ताश्चण्डांशोः पान्तु भानवः ॥१२९॥

चण्डांशोः खण्डितानेत्रकंजालिमंजुरंजनपंडिताः मण्डिताखिलदिक्प्रान्ताश्च भानवः पान्तु ।

May the rays of the sun protect you–the rays which are ingenious in giving sweet charm to the lotuses in the form of the eyes of खण्डिता ladies–the rays which brightened all the nooks and corners of the quarters.

शान्तविलासः

विशालविषयाटवीवलयलग्नदावानल-
प्रसृत्वरशिखावलीविकलितं मदीयं मनः ।
अमन्दमिलदिन्दिरे निखिलमाधुरीमन्दिरे
मुकुन्दमुखचन्दिरे चिरमिदं चकोरायताम् ॥१॥

अमन्द......चंदिरे इदं विशाल......मदीयं मनः चकोरायताम् ।

May my mind, which is distressed by the rows of flames, spreading around, of the forest conflagration which is burning the circle of the extensive forest in the form of the objects of senses (that surround me) act like the चकोर bird towards the moon in the form of the face of मुकुन्द, which is the receptacle of all sweetness and whose splendour is rapidly increasing.

अये जलधिनन्दिनीनयननीरजालम्बन
ज्वलज्ज्वलनजित्वरज्वरभरत्वराभङ्गुरम् ।
प्रभातजलजोन्नमद्गरिमगर्वसर्वङ्कषै-
र्जगत्त्रितयरोचनैः शिशिरयाशु मां लोचनैः ॥२॥

अये जलधिनन्दिनीनयननीरजालंबन (विष्णो) ज्वलज्ज्वलनजित्वरज्वरभरत्वरा-भंगुरं मां प्रभातजलजोन्नमद्गरिमगर्वसर्वंकषैः जगत्त्रितयरोचनैः लोचनैः आशु शिशिरय ।

O (God Vishnu), the support of the lotuses in the form of the eyes of Laxmi, speedily cool me, who am breaking under the force (त्वरा) of the excess of pain that conquers the burning fire, by your glances, liked by the three worlds, and the destroyers of the pride of greatness arising in a morning lotus.

स्मृतापि तरुणातपं करुणया हरन्ती नृणा-
मभङ्गुरतनुत्विषां वलयिता शतैर्विद्युताम् ।

कलिन्दनगनन्दिनीतटसुरद्रुमालम्बिनी
मदीयमतिचुम्बिनी भवतु कापि कादम्बिनी ॥३॥

स्मृता अपि (केवलं) करुणया नृणां तरुणातपं हरन्ती, अभङ्गुरतनुत्विषां विद्युतां शतैः वलयिता, कलिन्दनगनन्दिनीतटसुरद्रुमालम्बिनी, का अपि कादम्बिनी मदीयमतिचुम्बिनी भवतु ।

Let the indescribable row of clouds (श्रीकृष्ण) be the object of my contemplation, which, when merely remembered removes the terrible anguish through kindness, which is encircled by hundreds of lightnings of everlasting glow, which rests (is seated) on the celestial tree, (growing) on the bank of the daughter of the mountain कलिन्द.

कलिन्दनगनन्दिनीतटवनान्तरं भासय-
न्सदा पथि गतागतश्रमभरं हरन्प्राणिनाम् ।
लतावलिशतावृतो मधुरया रुचा संभृतो
ममाशु हरतु श्रमानतितरां तमालद्रुमः ॥४॥

कलिन्दनगनन्दिनीतटवनान्तरं भासयन् सदा प्राणिनां पथि गतागतश्रमभरं हरन्, लतावलिशतावृतः, मधुरया रुचा संभृतः, तमालद्रुमः आशु मम श्रमान् अतितरां हरतु ।

May the तमाल tree (श्रीकृष्ण) remove completely and instantly my fatigue—the tree which brightens the interior of the wilderness (वृन्दावन) on the banks of the (Jumna) daughter of the कलिन्द mountain, the tree which always removes the burden of the fatigue of going and coming in the journey (of travellers) (journey of births and deaths), the tree encircled by hundreds of rows of creepers (गोपीs) and adorned by the pleasant splendour,

जगज्जालं ज्योत्स्नामयनवसुधाभिर्जटिलय-
ञ्जनानां सन्तापं त्रिविधमपि सद्यः प्रशमयन् ।
श्रितो वृन्दारण्यं नतनिखिलवृन्दारकवृतो
मम स्वान्तध्वान्तं तिरयतु नवीनो जलधरः ॥५॥

First two lines the same. वृन्दारण्यं श्रितः नत...वृतः नवीनः जलधरः मम स्वान्तध्वान्तं तिरयतु ।

May the new cloud (श्रीकृष्ण) destroy the darkness of my heart, the cloud which pervades the surface of the world with the new nectar full of splendour, the cloud which instantaneously removes even the threefold troubles of the people, the cloud which inhabited the वृन्दावन forest and which was surrounded by all the Gods bowing down (to him)!

ग्रीष्मचण्डकरमण्डलभीष्म-
ज्वालसंसरणतापितमूर्तेः ।
प्रावृषेण्य इव वारिधरो मे
वेदनां हरतु वृष्णिवरेण्यः ॥६॥

वृष्णिवरेण्यः प्रावृषेण्यः इव वारिधरः ग्रीष्म......मूर्तेः मे वेदनां हरतु ।

May (श्रीकृष्ण) the best of (वृष्णिs) like the cloud in the rainy season, remove the agony of mine, (I) whose body is distressed by the terrible flames of the disc of the scorching summer-sun in the form of the worldly existence!

अपारे संसारे विषमविषयारण्यसरणौ
मम भ्रामं भ्रामं विगलितविरामं जडमतेः ।
परिश्रान्तस्यायं तरणितनयातीरनिलयः
समन्तात्सन्तापं हरिनवतमालस्तिरयतु ॥७॥

अपारे......सरणौ विगलितविरामं भ्रामं भ्रामं जडमतेः परिश्रान्तस्य मम समन्तात्सन्तापं अयं......तिरयतु ।

May this श्रीकृष्ण, the new तमाल tree, whose home is on the bank of the daughter of the sun, remove the encircling vexations of mine who am dull-minded, exhausted, and restlessly wandering often and often in this impassable worldly existence, which is a road to the uneven forest in the form of worldly pleasures!

आलिङ्गितो जलधिकन्यकया सलीलं
लग्नः प्रियङ्गुलतयेव तरुस्तमालः ।

देहावसानसमये हृदये मदीये
देवश्चकास्तु भगवानरविन्दनाभः ॥८॥

प्रियंगुलतया लग्नः तरुः तमालः इव सलीलं जलधिकन्यकया आलिंगितः देवः भगवान्, अरविन्दनाभः देहावसानसमये मदीये हृदये चकास्तु ।

May the divine God विष्णु (with a lotus at his naval) sportively embraced by the (delicate) daughter of the ocean, like the तमाल tree by the प्रियंगु creeper, shine in my heart at the time of the termination of (my) body !

नयनानन्दसन्दोहतुन्दिलीकरणक्षमा ।
तिरयत्वाशु सन्तापं कापि कादम्बिनी मम ॥९॥

नयना......क्षमा कापि कादम्बिनी आशु मम सन्तापं तिरयतु ।

May that indescribable row of clouds (श्रीकृष्ण) which is able to enhance the mass of joy to the eyes, immediately remove my mental agony !

वाचा निर्मलया सुधामधुरया यां नाथ शिक्षामदा-
स्तां स्वप्नेऽपि न संस्पृशाम्यहमहंभावावृतो निस्त्रपः ।
इत्यागःशतशालिनं पुनरपि स्वीयेषु मां बिभ्रत-
स्त्वत्तो नास्ति दयानिधिर्यदुपते मत्तो न मत्तोऽपरः ॥१०॥

हे यदुपते, नाथ सुधामधुरया निर्मलया वाचा यां शिक्षां (त्वं) अदाः तां अहं अहंभावावृतः निस्त्रपः च स्वप्नेऽपि न संस्पृशामि, इति आगःशतशालिनं मां पुनरपि स्वीयेषु बिभ्रतः त्वत्तः (अन्यः) दयानिधिः नास्ति, मत्तः अपरः मत्तः नास्ति ।

O Lord, the best of यदुs I, shameless and overwhelmed by ego, do not remember even in dream the advice you gave me by speech which was pure and as sweet as ambrosia. Thus although I have committed hundreds of faults, you consider me among your beloved creatures, there is no ocean of mercy other than you and no arrogant person other than myself.

पातालं व्रज याहि वा सुरपुरीमारोह मेरोः शिरः
पारावारपरम्परां तर तथाप्याशा न शान्तास्तव ।

आधिव्याधिपराहतो यदि सदा क्षेमं निजं वाञ्छसि
श्रीकृष्णेति रसायनं रसय रे शून्यैः किमन्यैः श्रमैः ॥११॥

Last line शून्यैः अन्यैः श्रमैः किम् others as they are.

Go to Patala, or to the city of Gods or ascend the top of the Meru, cross the line of oceans, yet your desires will not cease. Overpowered by mental and physical pains, if you desire eternal bliss (क्षेम), taste the elixir "श्रीकृष्ण"; why resort to other efforts which are fruitless!

गणिकाजामिलमुख्यानवता भवता बताहमपि ।
सीदन् भवमरुगर्ते करुणामूर्ते न सर्वथोपेक्ष्यः ॥१२॥

गणिकाजामिलमुख्यानवता भवता, भवमरुगर्ते सीदन् अहमपि हे करुणामूर्ते बत न सर्वथा उपेक्ष्यः ।

O mercy incarnate, Alas! you should not altogether neglect me, who am desponding in the desert of worldly existence, **You**-who protected sinners of whom गणिका and अजामिल are the chief.

मृद्वीका रसिता सिता समशिता स्फीतं निपीतं पयः
स्वर्यातेन सुधाप्यधायि कतिधा रम्भाधरः खण्डितः ।
सत्यं ब्रूहि मदीय जीव भवता भूयो भवे भ्राम्यता
कृष्णेत्यक्षरयोरयं मधुरिमोद्गारः क्वचिल्लक्षितः ॥१३॥

मृद्वीका...खण्डितः (तथापि) हे मदीय जीव त्वया भूयो भवे भ्राम्यता भवता कृष्णेत्यक्षरयोः अयं मधुरिमोद्गारः क्वचिल्लक्षितः (किम), सत्यं ब्रूहि ।

O my Soul, you have tasted the grapes, enjoyed sugar to your heart's desire, drunk ample milk, when you went to heaven, (how) many times did you drink (suck) nectar and bite the lower lip of रम्भा, yet, tell me the truth, did you anywhere in your wanderings in the transmigratory existence witness that stream of sweetness (which oozes) from the two letters of which the word कृष्ण consists ?

वज्रं पापमहीभृतां भवगदोद्रेकस्य सिद्धौषधं
मिथ्याज्ञाननिशाविशालतमसस्तिग्मांशुबिम्बोदयः ।

क्रूरक्लेशमहीरुहामुरुतरज्वालाजटालः शिखी
द्वारं निर्वृतिसद्मनो विजयते कृष्णेति वर्णद्वयम् ॥१४॥

Victorious indeed is the pair of letters "कृष्ण" which is a thunderbolt to the mountains in the form of sins, which is the specific medicine to the prolonged illness in the form of the worldly existence, which is the rise of the disc of the sun to the vast darkness of night in the form of errorneous knowledge, which is fire encircled by gigantic flames to the trees in the form of ruthless afflictions, which is the entrance to the palace of final beatitude.

रे चेतः कथयामि ते हितमिदं वृन्दावने चारय-
न्वृन्दं कोऽपि गवां नवाम्बुदनिभो बन्धुर्न कार्यस्त्वया ।
सौन्दर्यामृतमुद्गिरद्भिरभितः संमोह्य मन्दस्मितै-
रेष त्वां तव वल्लभांश्च विषयानाशु क्षयं नेष्यति ॥१५॥

रे चेत: इदं हितं ते कथयामि, वृन्दावने गवां वृन्दं चारयन् कोऽपि नवाम्बुदनिभ: बन्धुः त्वया न कार्य: । (यत:) एष: अभित: सौन्दर्यामृतमुद्गिरद्भि: मन्दस्मितैः संमोह्य, त्वां तव वल्लभान् च विषयान् आशु क्षयं नेष्यति ॥

O mind, I tell you this for your benefit–you should not form friendship with a certain person (कृष्ण) resembling a new cloud (in complexion) and feeding a herd of cows in the वृन्दावन forest. (For) He will entice you by his charming smiles emitting all around the nectar of his beauty and will quickly lead you and your fond objects to extinction (i.e. will liberate you from this transmigratory existence.)

अव्याख्येयां वितरति परां प्रीतिमन्तर्निमग्ना
कण्ठे लग्ना हरति नितरां यान्तरध्वान्तजालम् ।
तां द्राक्षाद्यैरपि बहुमतां माधुरीमुद्गिरन्तीं
कृष्णेत्याख्यां कथय रसने यद्यसि त्वं रसज्ञा ॥१६॥

(हे) रसने यदि त्वं रसज्ञा असि (तर्हि) या ('कृष्ण' इति आख्या) अन्तर्निमग्नां अव्याख्येयां परां प्रीतिं वितरति या कण्ठे लग्ना नितरां आन्तरध्वान्तजालं हरति, तां द्राक्षाद्यैरपि बहुमतां माधुरीं उद्गिरन्तीं " कृष्ण " इत्याख्यां कथय ।

O tongue, if your are an appreciator of sweetness, repeat that name "कृष्ण" giving out sweetness superior even to the grapes, which when it occupies the interior of the heart, gives inexplicable and great love (i. e. devotion) and which when repeated entirely removes the mass of internal darkness.

सन्त्येवास्मिञ्जगति बहवः पक्षिणो रम्यरूपा-
स्तेषां मध्ये मम तु महती वासना चातकेषु ।
यैरध्यक्षैरथ निजसखं नीरदं स्मारयद्भि-
श्चित्तारूढं भवति किमपि ब्रह्म कृष्णाभिधानम् ॥१७॥

अस्मिन् जगति बहवः रम्यरूपाः पक्षिणः सन्ति एव तेषां मध्ये चातकेषु मम तु महती वासना । यैः अध्यक्षैः अथ निजसखं नीरदं स्मारयद्भिः कृष्णाभिधानं किमपि ब्रह्म चित्तारूढं भवति ।

Many beautiful birds there are in this world; but among them all, I have a great fondness for चातक birds. (For) it is on account of them when they fall within the range of (my) sight and (consequently) remind (me) of their friend, cloud, that the indescribable ब्रह्म, named कृष्ण, rises (i. e. flashes) in my mind.

विष्वद्रीच्या भुवनमभितो भासते यस्य भासा
सर्वासामप्यहमिति विदां गूढमालम्बनं यः ।
तं पृच्छन्ति स्वहृदयमनावेदिनो विष्णुमन्या-
नन्यायोऽयं शिव शिव नृणां केन वा वर्णनीयः ॥१८॥

यस्य विष्वद्रीच्या भासा अखिलं भुवनं भासते, यः सर्वासां 'अहं' इति विदां गूढमालंबनम् । तं विष्णुं स्वहृदयं अनावेदिनः अन्यान् पृच्छन्ति । शिव शिव अयं नृणां अन्यायः केन वा वर्णनीयः ।

Alas ! who can describe the injustice of those men, who, not knowing their own hearts, inquire of others about विष्णु, by whose brilliance pervading the universe, the whole world shines and who is the incomprehensible basis of all knowledge of the consciousness of "अहं" (one's self).

सेवायां यदि साभिलाषमसि रे लक्ष्मीपतिः सेव्यतां
चिन्तायामसि सस्पृहं यदि तदा चक्रायुधश्चिन्त्यताम् ।
आलापं यदि कांक्षसि स्मररिपोर्गाथा तदालाप्यतां
स्वापं वाञ्छसि चेन्निरर्गलसुखे चेतः सुखं सुप्यताम् ॥१९॥

हे सखे चेत: यदि त्वं सेवायां साभिलाषं असि (तर्हि) लक्ष्मीपति: सेव्यताम् । चिन्तायां यदि सस्पृहं असि तदा चक्रायुध: चिन्त्यताम् । आलापं यदि कांक्षसि, तदा स्मररिपो: गाथा (त्वया) आलप्यताम् । स्वापं वांछसि चेत्, निरर्गलसुखे सुप्यताम् ।

O friend mind, if you desire to serve, serve the consort of लक्ष्मी; if you desire to contemplate, contemplate over विष्णु, (whose weapon is the disc). If you want to converse, sing the verses of शिव; if you want to sleep, sleep in unlimited joy (i. e. the joy of Brahma (ब्रह्म)).

भवग्रीष्मप्रौढातपनिवहसन्तप्तवपुषो
बलादुन्मूल्य द्राङ्निगडमविवेकव्यतिकरम् ।
विशुद्धेऽस्मिन्नात्मामृतसरसि नैराश्यशिशिरे
विगाहन्ते दूरीकृतकलुषजालाः सुकृतिनः ॥२०॥

दूरीकृतकलुषजाला: सुकृतिन: भवग्रीष्म...वपुष: द्राग् निगडं अविवेकव्यतिकरं बलात् उन्मूल्य अस्मिन् विशुद्धे नैराश्यशिशिरे आत्मामृतसरसि विगाहन्ते ।

Blessed persons, removing the net of the sin, with their bodies scorched by the excessive heat of the summer in the form of this world breaking immediately the chain of contact with ignorance, bathe in this excessively pure pond of the bliss of Atma, cool on account of hopelessness.

बन्धोन्मुक्त्यै खलु मखमुखान्कुर्वते कर्मपाशा-
नन्तःशान्त्यै मुनिशतमतानल्पचिन्तां भजन्ते ।
तीर्थे मज्जन्त्यशुभजलधेः पारमारोढुकामाः
सर्वं प्रामादिकमिह भवभ्रान्तिभाजां नराणाम् ॥२१॥

बन्धोन्मुक्त्यै खलु मखमुखान् कर्मपाशान् कुर्वते, अन्त:शान्त्यै मुनिशतमतानल्पचिन्तां भजन्ते, अशुभजलधे: पारमारोढुकामा: तीर्थे मज्जन्ति । भवभ्रान्तिभाजां नराणां इह सर्वं प्रामादिकं (विद्यते) ।

Everything done by persons, who are perplexed in this world, is erroneous. They perform a number of कर्मन्s (rites) of which the sacrifices are chief, for getting freedom from bondage, contemplate much over the opinions of hundreds of मुनिs (Sages) and bathe in holy places with a desire of crossing the sea of sins.

प्रथमं चुम्बितचरणा जङ्घाजानूरुनाभिहृदयानि ।
आश्लिष्य भावना मे खेलतु विष्णोर्मुखाब्जशोभायाम् ॥२२॥

मे भावना प्रथमं चुम्बितचरणा (पश्चात्) जंघाजानूरुनाभिहृदयानि आश्लिष्य विष्णोर्मुखाब्जशोभायां खेलतु ।

May my imagination sport on the splendour of the lotus-like face of विष्णु, after first kissing (contemplating over) the feet and then embracing (contemplating) the legs, the knees, the thighs, the naval and the chest !

मलयानिलकालकूटयो रमणीकुन्तलभोगिभोगयोः
श्वपचात्मभुवोर्निरन्तरा मम भूयात्परमात्मनि स्थितिः ॥२३॥

मलयानिलकालकूटयोः (निरन्तरा) रमणीकुन्तलभोगिभोगयोः (निरन्तरा) श्वपचात्मभुवोः (निरन्तरा)(ईदृशी) परमात्मनि स्थितिः मे भूयात् ।

May I experience the residence in the great soul (unity with it), where one sees non-difference between the breeze coming from the मलय mountain and the deadly poison, between the hair of a beautiful woman and the body of a serpent and between Chandal and Cupid.

निखिलं जगदेव नश्वरं
पुनरस्मिन्नितरां कलेवरम् ।
अथ तस्य कृते कियानयं
क्रियते हन्त जनैः परिश्रमः ॥२४॥

निखिलं जगदेव नश्वरं, पुनः अस्मिन् (जगति) कलेवरं नितरां (नश्वरं), हन्त । अथ तस्य (कलेवरस्य) कृते कियानयं परिश्रमः जनैः क्रियते ।

The very whole universe is transitory and in it much more so is our body; alas ! What great troubles are undergone by men for its sake ?

प्रतिपलमखिलाँल्लोकान्मृत्युमुखं प्रविशतो निरीक्ष्यापि ।
हा हन्त किमिति चित्तं विरमति नाद्यापि विषयेभ्यः ॥२५॥

प्रतिपल...चित्तं किमिति अद्यापि विषयेभ्यः न विरमति ।

Even after marking every moment all people entering the jaws of Death yet alas! why does not mind desist from the worldly objects ?

सपदि विलयमेतु राज्यलक्ष्मी-
रुपरि पतन्त्वथवा कृपाणधाराः ।
अपहरतुतरां शिरः कृतान्तो
मम तु मतिर्न मनागपैतु धर्मात् ॥२६॥

Let royal splendour vanish all at once, or let sword-edges fall over (my body). The God of Death may better take away my head but let not my mind (i. e. thought) budge an inch (lit. a little) from duty.

अपि बहलदहनजालं मूर्ध्नि रिपुर्मे निरन्तरं धमतु ।
पातयतु वासिधारामहमणुमात्रं न किञ्चिदपभाषे ॥२७॥

मे रिपुः (मे) मूर्ध्नि निरन्तरं बहलदहनजालमपि धमतु, वा असिधारां पातयतु, अहमणुमात्रं न किञ्चिद् अपभाषे ।

Let my enemy incessantly blow excessive fire on my head or fall the edge of the sword (on it), I shall not talk even one offensive word.

तरणोपायमपश्यन्नपि मामक जीव ताम्यसि कुतस्त्वम् ।
चेतःसरणावस्यां किं नागन्ता कदापि नन्दसुतः ॥२८॥

हे मामक जीव तरणोपायं अपश्यन्नपि त्वं कुतः ताम्यसि, अस्यां चेतः-सरणौ नन्दसुतः कदापि न आगन्ता किम् ।

O my soul, though not conversant with any means to save (yourself) why do you pine? Will the son of Nanda (Krishna) never (come into the way of your mind) be remembered by you ?

श्रियो मे मा सन्तु क्षणमपि च माद्यद्गजघटा-
मदभ्राम्यद्भृङ्गावलिमधुरझङ्कारसुभगाः ।
निमग्नानां यासु द्रविणमदिराघूर्णितदृशां
सपर्यासौकर्यं हरिचरणयोरस्तमयते ॥२९॥

क्षणमपि च माद्यद्गजघटामदभ्राम्यद्भृङ्गावलिमधुरझंकारसुभगाः श्रियः मे मा सन्तु, यासु निमग्नानां द्रविणमदिराघूर्णितदृशां (नराणां) हरिचरणयोः सपर्यासौकर्यं अस्तम् अयते ।

May I not even for a moment possess the wealth which is attractive owing to the humming of the row of bees, hovering over the rut of the crowds of (rutting) elephants; because in the case of the people merged in लक्ष्मी the ease of worship of the feet of Hari disappears owing to their eyesight rolling (frenzied) through the wine in the form of wealth.

किं निःशङ्कं शेषे शेषे वयसः समागतो मृत्युः ।
अथवा सुखं शयीथा निकटे जागर्ति जाह्नवी जननी ॥३०॥

वयसः शेषे किं निःशंकं शेषे (यतः) मृत्युः समागतः । अथवा, सुखं शयीथाः (यतः) निकटे जननी जाह्नवी जागर्ति ।

Why do you sleep fearlessly in the remaining part of (your) life as death has arrived ? Or sleep happily as the mother Ganges is awake near (you).

सन्तापयामि किमहं धावं धावं धरातले हृदयम् ।
अस्ति मम शिरसि सततं नन्दकुमारः प्रभुः परमः ॥३१॥

धरातले धावं धावं किमहं हृदयं सन्तापयामि । (यतः) मम शिरसि सततं परमः प्रभुः नन्दकुमारः अस्ति ।

Why do I torment my heart by running frequently (after every thing) on the surface of the earth ? The Supreme Lord, the son of नन्द, is there always over my head (i. e. to rescue me).

रे रे मनो मम मनोभवशासनस्य
पादाम्बुजद्वयमनारतमानमन्तम् ।

किं मां निपातयसि संसृतिगर्तमध्ये
नैतावता तव गमिष्यति पुत्रशोकः ॥३२॥

रे रे मम मनः मनोभवशासनस्य पादाम्बुजद्वयं अनारतं आनमन्तं मां संसृतिगर्तमध्ये किं निपातयसि। एतावता तव पुत्रशोकः न गमिष्यति।

O my mind, why do you hurl me into the pit of the transmigratory existence--me who am incessantly bowing down at the lotus-like feet of the slayer of the mind-born (your son-Cupid)? By doing this much your grief for the loss of your son will not cease.

मरकतमणिमेदिनीधरो वा
तरुणतरस्तरुरेष वा तमालः।
रघुपतिमवलोक्य तत्र दूरा-
दृषिनिकरैरिति संशयः प्रपेदे ॥३३॥

तत्र दूराद् रघुपतिं अवलोक्य एषः मरकतमणिमेदिनीधरः वा तरुणतरः तमालः तरुः इति ऋषिनिकरैः संशयः प्रपेदे॥

There (in the दण्डकारण्य) at the sight of the lord of रघुs from a distance, a doubt was entertained by the groups of sages as to whether it was a mountain of emeralds or a young तमाल tree.

तरणितनया किं स्यादेषा न तोयमयी हि सा
मरकतमणिज्योत्स्ना वा स्यान्न सा मधुरा कुतः।
इति रघुपतेः कायच्छाया विलोकनतत्परै-
रुदितकुतुकैः कैः कैरादौ न संदिदिहे जनैः ॥३४॥

एषा तरणितनया स्यात् किम्? न, सा हि तोयमयी; वा मरकतमणि-ज्योत्स्ना स्यात्? न, सा कुतः (ईदृशी) मधुरा? इति विलोकनतत्परैः उदितकुतुकैः कैः कैः जनैः आदौ रघुपतेः कायच्छाया न सन्दिदिहे? (सर्वैरेव सन्दिदिहे इति अर्थः।)

Is this possibly the daughter of the Sun? No. She, indeed, is full of water; or is this the lustre of emerald? No. How can it be so pleasant? What persons were there, who, being curiously absorbed in observation, did not mistake the complexion of the body of the lord of रघुs (for यमुना etc.) thus?

चपला जलदाच्च्युता लता वा
तरुमुख्यादिति संशये निमग्नः ।
गुरुनिःश्वसितैः कपिर्मनीषी
निरणैषीदथ तां वियोगिनीति ॥३५॥

जलदात् च्युता चपला (इयं) वा तरुमुख्यात् च्युता लता (इयं) इति संशये निमग्नः मनीषी कपिः अथ गुरुनिःश्वसितैः तां (सीतां) वियोगिनी इति निरणैषीत् ।

The wise monkey (हनुमान) entertained doubts like "Is this the lightning dropped down from a cloud ? or a creeper dropped from a celestial tree ? Afterwards, he ascertained that she was a वियोगिनी lady (i. e. सीता) from her deep long sighs.

भूतिर्नीचगृहेषु विप्रसदने दारिद्र्यकोलाहलो
नाशो हन्त सतामसत्पथजुषामायुः समानां शतम् ।
दुर्नीतिं तव वीक्ष्य कोपदहनज्वालाजटालोऽपि सन्.
किं कुर्वे जगदीश यत्पुनरहं दीनो भवानीश्वरः ॥३६॥

First two lines, the same. हे जगदीश, तव दुर्नीतिं वीक्ष्य कोपदहनज्वालाजटालोऽपि सन् अहं किं कुर्वे ? यद् अहं दीनः भवान् पुनः ईश्वरः ।

There is prosperity (reigning) in the houses of the wicked, (while) in the house of a Brahmin there is the uproar of poverty, also ! the good are ruined (while) followers of an evil path have a life of a hundred years (in store for them). O Lord of this world, although I am filled with the flames of the fire in the form of anger, at the sight of this injustice of yours, what shall I do, since I am a pauper, whereas you are the lord ?

आ मूलाद्रत्नसानोर्मलयवलयितादा च कूलात्पयोधे-
र्यावन्तः सन्ति काव्यप्रणयनपटवस्ते विशङ्कं वदन्तु ।
मृद्वीकामध्यनिर्यन्मसृणरसझरीमाधुरीभाग्यभाजां
वाचामाचार्यतायाः पदमनुभवितुं कोऽस्ति धन्यो मदन्यः ॥३७॥

रत्नसानोः मूलात् आ मलयवलयितात् पयोधेः च कूलात् आ यावन्तः काव्यप्रणयनपटवः सन्ति ते निःशङ्कं वदन्तु। मृद्वीका...भाजां वाचां आचार्यतायाः पदं अनुभवितुं मदन्यः कः धन्यः अस्ति।

Let all those declare undoubtedly—those who are well-versed in composing poems, (those living) from the foot of the Meru mountain down to the shores of the Ocean, encircled by the Malaya Mountain, if there is any blessed person other than myself (blessed enough) to experience the position (or dignity) of being the master of words, possessed of the fortune of having the sweetness of the flow of the sweet juice, issuing out of the interior of grapes.

गिरां देवी वीणागुणरणनहीनादरकरा
यदीयानां वाचाममृतमयमाचामति रसम् ।
वचस्तस्याकर्ण्य श्रवणसुभगं पण्डितपते-
रधुन्वन्मूर्धानं नृपशुरथवायं पशुपतिः ॥३८॥

वीणागुणरणनहीनादरकरा गिरां देवी यदीयानां वाचां अमृतमयं रसं आचामति तस्य पण्डितपतेः श्रवणसुभगं वचः आकर्ण्य मूर्धानं अधुन्वन् अयं नृपशुः अथवा पशुपतिः (विद्यते)।

He must be either शिव or a beast in the form of a man who does not nod his head on hearing the poems (lit. speech) of the lord of poets (i. e. जगन्नाथपण्डित himself) charming to the ears–(the lord of poets) the sentiment of whose poetical composition, full of nectar, the goddess of speech sips, suffering her hand to disregard the playing upon the chords of her lute.

मधु द्राक्षा साक्षादमृतमथ वामाधरसुधा
कदाचित्केषांचिन्न खलु विदधीरन्नपि मुदम् ।
ध्रुवं ते जीवन्तोऽप्यहह मृतका मन्दमतयो
न येषामानन्दं जनयति जगन्नाथभणितिः ॥३९॥

First two lines–the same. जगन्नाथभणितिः येषां आनन्दं न जनयति अहह ! ते मन्दमतयः जीवन्तः अपि ध्रुवं मृतकाः (सन्ति)।

Honey, grapes, nectar itself and also the nectar on the lower lips of lovely ladies may not give delight even to some on some occasions (कदाचित्). But alas! those dull persons in whom the poems of Jagannath do not produce delight, are really dead, though (they are) living.

निर्माणे यदि मार्मिकोऽसि नितरामत्यन्तपाकद्रवन्-
मृद्वीकामधुमाधुरीमदपरीहारोद्धुराणां गिराम् ।
काव्यं तर्हि सखे सुखेन कथय त्वं संमुखे मादृशां
नो चेद् दुष्कृतमात्मना कृतमिव स्वान्ताद्बहिर्मा कृथाः ॥४०॥

If you are exceedingly capable of composing (words) poems which are successful in removing the pride of the sweetness of juice dropping from the grapes which are fully ripe, then, friend, you may, with pleasure, sing your poem before me; if not, do not show it outside your own heart, like a sinful act committed by you.

मद्वाणि मा कुरु विषादमनादरेण
मात्सर्यमग्नमनसां सहसा खलानाम् ।
काव्यारविन्दमकरन्दमधुव्रताना-
मास्येषु धास्यसितमां कियतो विलासान् ॥४१॥

O my speech, do not be desponding because of the disrespect shown towards you by the wicked whose minds are full of jealousy because you will create immense pleasure on the faces of those, who are like bees to the honey in the lotus in the form of poetry.

विद्वांसो वसुधातले परवचःश्लाघासु वाचंयमा
भूपालाः कमलाविलासमदिरोन्मीलन्मदाघूर्णिताः ।
आस्ये धास्यति कस्य लास्यमधुना धन्यस्य कामालस-
स्वर्वामाधरमाधुरीमधरयन् वाचां विपाको मम ॥४२॥

वसुधातले विद्वांसः परवचःश्लाघासु वाचंयमाः (सन्ति) भूपालाः कमलाविलासमदिरोन्मीलन्मदाघूर्णिताः (सन्ति), अधुना कामालसस्वर्वामा...धरयन् मम वाचां विपाकः कस्य धन्यस्य आस्ये लास्यं धास्यति ।

On the surface of the Earth (in this world) the learned people are very sparing in praising the poems of others; the kings are staggering with the intoxication arising from the wine in the form of the pleasures of wealth. Now, on whose face, will the best poetry of mine, which surpasses the sweetness of the lowerlip of the impassioned heavenly damsels, dance? (i. e. those who will enjoy my poetry will be really blessed.)

धुर्यैरपि माधुर्यैर्द्राक्षाक्षीरेक्षुमाक्षिकसुधानाम् ।
वन्द्यैव माधुरीयं पण्डितराजस्य कवितायाः ॥४३॥

द्राक्षाक्षीरेक्षु...सुधानाम् धुर्यैः माधुर्यैः अपि पण्डितराजस्य कवितायाः इयं माधुरी वन्द्या एव ।

The sweetness of the verses of the prince of poets (जगन्नाथ himself) is really praiseworthy even to the best sweetness of grapes, milk, sugarcane, honey and nectar.

शास्त्राण्याकलितानि नित्यविधयः सर्वेऽपि सम्भाविता
दिल्लीवल्लभपाणिपल्लवतले नीतं नवीनं वयः ।
संप्रत्युज्झितवासनं मधुपुरीमध्ये हरिः सेव्यते
सर्वं पण्डितराजराजितिलकेनाकारि लोकाधिकम् ॥४४॥

शास्त्राणि आकलितानि, सर्वेऽपि नित्यविधयः संभाविताः, दिल्लीवल्लभपाणिपल्लवतले नवीनं वयः नीतम्। मधुपुरीमध्ये हरिः उज्झितवासनं सेव्यते । (एवं) पण्डितराजराजितिलकेन सर्वं लोकाधिकं अकारि ।

The shastras were mastered; all the usual duties also were attended to; the prime of life was led under the blossomlike hands of the king of Delhi. Now, Vishnu is being worshipped (by me) in the city of Muttra in a manner in which all the desires are given up. (Thus) everything extraordinary has been done by (me), the foremost of the lines of the princes of poets.

दुर्वृत्ता जारजन्मानो हरिष्यन्तीति शङ्कया ।
मदीयपद्यरत्नानां मञ्जूषैषा कृता मया ॥४५॥

"जारजन्मानः दुर्वृत्ताः हरिष्यन्ति" इति शंकया मया एषा मदीयपद्यरत्नानां मंजूषा कृता ।

I have made this box (a safe, as it were) of the precious stones in the form of my verses, through the fear of their being plagiarised (i.e. stolen away) by the people of bad conduct and born of paramours.

Notes

1. माधुर्यस्य परमा सीमा-माधुर्यपरमसीमा the highest limit of sweetness. सारस्वतं एव जलधि:-कर्म तस्य मथनं-तस्मात् संभूता न अल्पं अनल्पम्–अनल्पं सुखं ददाति इति-उ त. । सुधा इव कविता-सुधा-कविता--कर्म. This way of opening a book will indeed seem unusual, but it is not strange in the case of जगन्नाथपंडित who indulged rather too much in self-praise as we shall see later on. It should also be noted in connection with this verse that it is not found in any other edition except that of Mr. Vaidya, which we are following and may probably be an interpolation.

2. करटिन्-formed by the affix इन् showing possession. करटः अस्ति अस्य. Here करट is used in the sense of a temple of an elephant. " काकेभगण्डौ करटौ " मदेन मलिनाःगण्डाः येषां तेः(बहु.). The elephant's rutting in the prime of youth is proverbial and has been referred to several times by the Sanskrit poets. दिशां अन्ताः-दिगन्ताः । करिणी-means a female elephant. They are by very nature objects of pity. कारुण्यस्य आस्पदं, by rule पात्र आस्पद स्थान etc. (vide Apte's guide sec 11–b) which requires these words to be used always in the neu. gender Sing. number. मृग्यन्ते (व्याधैः) इति मृगा. Beasts of prey. Ordinary beasts of prey are not worthy of even being attacked by the lion because they are insignificant. नखानां पाण्डित्यं the prowess of his nails which are extraordinarily sharp. नास्त्युपमा येषां ते अनुपमा –अनुपमाः शिखाः येषां–तेषाम्–of unparalleled sharpness.

The lion here complains that throughout the length and breadth of the world there is no animal that can match him in valour.

This type of verses is technically called an अन्योक्ति or अप्रस्तुतप्रशंसा. अप्रस्तुतप्रशंसा या सा सैव प्रस्तुताश्रया (K. Pr. 10–15) i. e. description of what is not the matter in hand, leading to the implication of the matter in hand. For example in the present verse the poet expresses the invincibility of the lion, implying thereby his (the poet's) unique accomplishments in the sphere of poetry, polemics (science of discussion) and his versatility in all shastras. मंमट further sub-divides this अप्रस्तुतप्रशंसा in five sections, which does not form the province of the present course of studies. Some think-and that very correctly perhaps that herein जगन्नाथ pandit gives free vent to his egoistic nature, which is amply corroborated when we refer to many of his other verses (See introduction.) Leaving aside modesty, which a learned man must avoid, he waxes eloquent in praising his own unique accomplishments and vast erudition.

Idea:—The elephant is sorry because he has no match.

Application—Extra-ordinary persons feel uneasy when they do not find a competitor to fight with them.

3. मानस is the conventional abode of राजहंस (vide मेघदूत पूर्वमेघ latter half of v. 11 आकैलासाद् etc.) विकचानि च तानि सारसानि तेषामालयः ताभ्यः स्खलन्तः ये परागाः तैः सुरभीकृतं, adj. of पयः अभूततद्भावे च्विः (by Pan. 5-4–50), मिलतां अनेकेषां भेकानां कुलैः

आकुलम्–तस्मिन्-adj. of पल्वलजलम् मरालानां कुलानां नायकः ' परागः कौसुमे रेणौ ". " पल्वलं चाल्पसरः " Herein the contrast is very effectively brought out by placing the crystalline and highly scented waters enjoyed in the मानस, side by side with the filthy water of a puddle, repulsive owing to the shrill croaking of frogs.

Idea:—How is it possible for a person once rolling in luxuries to live in adversity ?

Appli:—This is applicable to a person who was once affluent (rich) but now indigent (poor).

Cf. सुखात्तु यो याति नरो दरिद्रतां धृतः शरीरेण मृतः स जीवति (M. K. 1–10).

4. तृष्णया लोले विलोचने यस्य सः adj. to चकोरीगणे। प्रस्थातुं कामः यस्य सः adj. to माने. For the compound see Apte's guide Sec. 181. धाराणां धराः तेषां आडम्बरः। ' आडम्बरः समारम्भे ' इति विश्वः। Here are four locative absolute constructions. It is a convention of Sanskrit poets that the चकोरी birds long for drinking the rays of the moon. कैरव is a night-lotus which blooms at the appearance of the moon. The bud of a lotus resembles a closed mouth and hence the poet naturally likens this opening of the bud to that of the mouth.

The rise of the moon causes the disappearance of the anger of proud ladies, provoked by the jealousy in love as the moon infuses love in the heart of ladies so effectively that they are compelled to forget their anger.

Cf. for the conventions about चकोर and कैरव and the idea in the third line.

शृङ्गारदीक्षामणिः ... ...
... चकोरपरिषच्चिन्तामणिश्चन्द्रमाः ॥ प्रसन्न 7–60
स्वैरं कैरवकोरकान् विदलयन् यूनां मनः खेदय-
न्नम्भोजानि निमीलयन् मृगदृशां मानं समुन्मूलयन् ।
... ... इन्दुः समुज्जृम्भते ॥ प्रसन्न 7–59

धाराधराडंबरः विधातुमुचितः Here the infinitive is used in the passive sense. cf. उचितः प्रणयो वरं विहन्तुं M. 3–3.

Idea:—It does not become the creator to cover up the moon when so many are longing for its appearance.

Appli:—It is not proper for a prosperous man to nip in the bud, for nothing, the hopes of future prospects of the humble.

5. निरपेक्षः (विद्यते) v. l. स्पन्दमानं. meaning "throbbing" is not so appealing.

दलञ्च तदरविन्दं च तस्य संबोधनम् । गन्धं वहति. the conveyer of fragrance i. e. wind. निर्गता अपेक्षा यस्मात् सः–निरपेक्षः मञ्जु is used here adverbially. अन्य the other or here it may mean extraordinary cf. अन्या जगद्धितमयी मनसः प्रवृत्तिः etc, तावकीन–is an adjective from युष्मद् formed according to तवकममकावेकवचने (Pan 4-3-3). "विमर्दोत्थे परिमलो गन्धो जनमनोहरे" मलते धारयति जनमनांसीति परिमलः परिमल is so called because it attracts the minds of the people. "अनुनये तु अयि" The particle अयि is used for gentle address. Also see. Bh V–1–10.

Idea:—The wind, unlike the bee, is the disinterested friend of the lotus.

Appli:—It is necessary to learn to understand the real worth of persons who hover around us, humming our panegyrics, with a view to the achievement of their selfish ends, and those noble minded, selfless souls who utilize their life for the good of others. Here bees represent selfish persons and wind the selfless one.

6. कुटज is a kind of flower growing on the summits of mountains (Meghduta 1-4) मा गा:-मा अगा: मा or मा स्म in the prohibitive sense is used with the aorist in the imperative sense, the augment अ being dropped. cf. क्लैब्यं मास्म गम: पार्थ। (B. G. 2-3) मधु करोति तच्छील: इति मधुकर: मकरन्देन तुंदिला: (corpulent) " मास्म माऽलं च वारणे". The कुटज is an insignificant flower and it is consequently a great honour done to it if a bee, greatly respected by the lotuses, sanctifies it by its visit.

Idea :--O Kutaja do not disrespect the bee.

Appli : –It is an excellent piece of advice to an ordinary man wherein he is asked not to lose the splendid opportunity of treating a dignified guest who was once extremely honoured by the great persons although he has come to him at that time as a mendicant.

7. वनस्य अन्तरम्-in the heart of the forest and not अन्यद् वनं as usual. मिलन्त्य: अलिमाला: यस्मिन् स: adj. to रसाला: "आम्रश्चूतो रसाल:" Hence विरसान्-विगुणान्-Dull, without any interest. According to convention of poets, the कोकिल and the आम्रवृक्ष are closely connected for which cf. चूताङ्कुरास्वादकषायकण्ठ: पुंस्कोकिलो यन्मधुरं चुकूज। मनस्विनीमानविघातदक्षं तदेव जातं वचनं स्मरस्य॥ (K. S. 3–32) The cuckoo when alone is prohibited from cooing by the Sanskrit poets in general lest it be harassed by the crows through natural antipathy. When a mango tree blossoms

generally all cuckoos flock there and enjoy by cooing. At that time they unitedly will be able to withstand the attacks of the crows. For the antipathy of the cuckoos and crows cf. Bh. V 1-25. The crows are so dull that they cannot recognise the cuckoos unless they coo. If the second interpretation i.e. अन्यत् वनम् is followed the danger of the cuckoos being harassed by crows remains as it is. Here यावत् means "Until" cf. स्तन्यत्यागं यावत् पुत्रयोरवेक्षस्व । U. 7.

Idea:—O cuckoo, pass your days quietly until a mango blossoms.

Appli:—One should bear with the apathetic circumstances until fortune favours him.

कमलिनी-कमलानि सन्ति अस्याः—a lotus plant, मलिनीकरोषि soil, a verb formed by च्वि formation (न मलिनं अमलिनं, अमलिनं संपद्यमानं करोषि) "मकरन्दः पुष्परसः" न अभिजानन्ति इति अनभिज्ञाः-non-conversant, ignorant. परिणतः च असौ मकरन्दः च तस्य मार्मिकाः appreciators of developed honey. चिरं आयुः येषां ते-long lived.

Idea:—The कमलिनी should not repent because it is disrespected by herons.

Appli:—meritorious man, why are you sorry if you are disrespected by fools ? As long as the learned who appreciate your merit are alive, you have gained every thing.

9. The beauty of this verse depends upon the natural puns on the words नीच, रस, etc. and the cousequent implied senses to which it leads, अत्यन्तं, सरसं हृदयं यस्य सः-अत्यन्तसरसहृदयः । बहु॰ परेषां गुणग्रहीता—This is the example of a सापेक्षसमास, सापेक्षत्वेऽपि गमकत्वात्समासः ।

Although there is an अपेक्षा (need) of a compound the compound is not formed. Here गुण ought to have been connected with परेषां as परगुणग्रहीता, But even though it is not connected, this सापेक्षसमास indicates that while interpreting the words we cannot but understand it as one समास though according to actual words परेषां is away from गुणग्रहीता. गुणानां ग्रहीता-गुणग्रहीता ष. त. मा कृथाः for this construction see मा गाः (Bh. V. I-6).

The following are the principal puns नीच (1) low (2) poor. हृदय (1) bottom (2) Heart. रस (1) water (2) love. ग्रहीता (1) acceptor (2) appreciator. गुण (1) Rope to draw water (2) merit.

Idea:—O well, do not be disheartened because you are deep, the people are bound to come to you as they want fresh water which you possess in abundance. The idea with reference to the person, "Do not get dejected because you are poor, other people are bound to seek you as you have sincerity of love and appreciation for their merits".

Appli:—O man, never be sorry with the thought 'I am exceedingly poor (नीच); because your heart is full of love (रस) and you are the appreciator (ग्रहीता) of merits (गुण) of others.

अमन्दः मरन्दः यस्मिन् तत–बहु. adj. to अरविन्दम्, दलत्च तदरविन्दं च –कर्म० " हा विषादजुगार्तिषु " The tragic element is obvious since the bee, who passed his days once in a paradise as it were, in the form of the lotus incessantly dripping with honey, is now pursuing the mean desire of resorting to a कुटज.

Idea:—How does a bee long for a कुटज flower ?

Appli.:—The poet is annoyed at the sight of a man who once passed his days rolling in luxuries, now stooping before his perverse fortune and yielding to degenerating conduct. He expects him to break, never to bend before misfortunes.

The idea is parallel to—

वरं विभवहीनेन प्राणैः संतर्पितोऽनलः ।

नोपचारपरिभ्रष्टः कृपणः प्रार्थितो जनः । सुभाषितम्.

11. गिरां विषयः अस्तु may be the subject of speech i. e. who will describe your greatness. फणिन्–a serpent. पुष्टि पुष् to nourish. उद् + गॄ to vomit. उद्गिरतः genitive sing. of the present participle of the above root. परिमलस्य उद्गाराः–outpourings of fragrance.

Idea:—O Sandal, none is able to describe your greatness.

Appli.:—This refers to persons mad with an inordinate desire for charity, even towards those who deserve immediate annihilation, being a bane to society.

12. उरीकृ–to imitate–to accept " ऊरर्यूरी चोररी च विस्तारेऽङ्गीकृतौ त्रयम्" पटीयस् expert. पुष्टिं तनोषि bring fragrance to पिंषन् reducing to atoms, grinding

Idea:—O Sandal, none can imitate your generosity.

Appli.:—This refers to too good people of the type of शंकर, who do not refuse to give even a self-destructive boon to their enemies. They cannot overcome their nature which is goodness unalloyed.

13. नीरं च क्षीरं च (द्वंद्व) तयोः विवेकः–तस्मिन् in separating milk from water, which is the peculiar characteristic

of the swans. cf. हंसः श्वेतो बकः श्वेतः को भेदो बकहंसयोः। नीरक्षीर-विभागे तु हंसो हंसः बको बकः॥ आलस्यं तनुषे become lazy. कुलव्रतम् a vow handed down from one generation to another. cf. गलितवयसामिक्ष्वाकूणामिदं हि कुलव्रतम्। R. V. 3–70. विश्व is treated as a pronoun and hence the loc is विश्वस्मिन् and not विश्वे.

Idea:—O swan don't leave your hereditary characteristics.

Appli:—If the leaders of society themselves set at naught their own hereditary duties, none of the followers also will abide by his duty.

14. करवालस्य धारायाः इव आकारः येषां ते (बहु.)-similar in form to the blade of a sword. 'कौक्षेयको मण्डलाग्रः करवालः" क्राः=क्रूरतराः here. पुमान् गौः पुंगवः the best of cows. भुजंगमेषु पुंगवा (स. त.) " स्युरुत्तरपदे व्याघ्रपुङ्गवर्षभकुञ्जराः। सिंहशार्दूलनागाद्याः पुंसि श्रेष्ठार्थगोचराः " द्राक्षाणां दीक्षायां गुरवः who are fit to become preceptors to teach sweetness to grapes. केऽपि indescribable. See Bh. V. I. 5.

Appli:—This refers to persons who are outwardly quite apathetic but inwardly very sympathetic.

15. स्वस्य छन्दः यथा स्यात्तथा स्वच्छन्दम् (अव्य.). अन्याः हरितः हरिदन्तराणि other quarters. ' दिशश्च ककुभः काष्ठा आशाश्च हरितश्च ताः " दलत्-blooming अथ but. if. for the use, vide यदि यथा वदति क्षितिपस्तथा त्वमसि किं पितुरुत्कुलया त्वया। अथ तु वेत्सि शुचिव्रतमात्मनः पतिकुले तव दास्यमपि क्षमम्॥ शाकुं. 5–27.

Idea:—Wind is not a selfish parasite like bees.

16. निदाघे (in summer) मिहिरस्य (sun) ज्वालानां शतैः-निदाघमिहिरज्वालाशतैः। नितरां दह्यन्तेऽत्र इति निदाघः। " निदाघ उष्णोपगम उष्ण ऊष्मागमस्तपः " पांथानां संततिः a line of travellers. संतापस्य मालाभिः आकुला perturbed by continuous heat. निर्गतं अन्तरं यस्य सः adj. to आधिः-तस्य पटलैः (by constant mental anguish).

चिद् sometimes takes the nom. मयि याते loc absolute construction गन्ता 3rd pers. sing of the first future of गम्.

Idea :—Even though oceans have a tremendously great stock of water, yet it is of no use to people in general.

Appli.:—Even the life of the poor who get emaciated by the sincere thought of sympathy for others in their miseries is for better than that of the rich who do not give vent to such feelings.

17. पतङ्गाः birds. "पतङ्गौ पक्षिसूर्यौ च" संकोचम् अञ्चति literally means getting contracted. अम्बरस्य पन्थाः अम्बरपथः formed irregularly by ऋक्पूरब्धूः पथामानक्षे (Pan. 5-4-74) दीनदीनः utterly miserable. The repetition here shows the intensity of meaning. कतमां गतिं अभ्युपैतु is a question for which no other adequate answer can be found out except that he should fall a victim to death. रसाल means a mango tree. " आम्रश्चूतो रसालोऽसौ " हन्त. Alas ! " हन्त हर्षेऽनुकम्पायाम् "

Idea :—What should a fish do, when the pond is dried up ?

Appli.:—Here is described the utter helplessness of a miserable servant, in contrast with those fortunate ones who have shelter elsewhere, when their master is in adversity.

18. अम्बुजिनि O lotus-plant. मा अमंस्था : don't consider, don't show. अस्मिन् मारुते सौरभलोभं मा अमंस्थाः is interpreted in two ways (1) Don't think that the wind is greedy after your fragrance (like the bee), (2) Don't be greedy in giving your fragrance to the wind, as you feel when you give it to the bee. Both these are correct

and supported by commentators. मुद् (noun) pleasure. महित:-greatly honoured आत्मा-self. अर्थितानी-to reduce to the condition of a beggar.

Appli. (1) A donor should not hesitate to give money to a self-less person. (2) Disgusted with selfish persons donors sometimes bar their door even to the unselfish.

19. वदान्येषु गुरवः (स. त.) The best of the generous. " स्युर्वदान्यस्थूललक्ष्यदानशौण्डा बहुप्रदे " मिलिन्दे मञ्जु गुञ्जति loc. abso. Construction. मौनं मा उपयासीः Don't become silent. सुरतरवः-desire-yielding trees. They are enumerated in the verse पञ्चैते देवतरवो मन्दारः पारिजातकः । सन्तानः कल्पवृक्षश्चपुंसि वा हरिचन्दनम् ॥ Bearing the bees on the head is the highest honour that can be given to them and hence it would be improper for Malati to treat them with indifference. **Idea :**—O मालति, don't treat the bee with indifference. **Appli.** It is not proper to treat a distinguished guest with indifference.

20. द्वे जिह्वे येषां तैः (बहु) According to the Indian Mythology the tongue of the snake was cut into two when he liked the Darbha grass on which the pot of ambrosia was placed. (vide Mbh. Adi. 27-34) गुण-गण-वान्-possessed of multitudes of merit. सतां असेव्यतां नीतः rendered useless for being the shelter of the good. औन्नत्यं-greatness. किं कथयामः we cannot adequately describe. " द्विजिह्वौ सर्पसूचकौ" द्विजिह्व-a serpent, a traducer.

Idea:—O sandal, how should we describe your goodness ?

Appli:—It is suggested by the meaning of द्विजिह्व. Even though traducers ruin the reputation of good persons, they are not chastised by them, which is indeed, an indication of their extra-ordinary goodness.

21. मधु पिबतीति (उप. त.) गहनम्–a forest विटपिन् lit. one having branches i. e. a tree "विटपी पादपस्तरुः" प्रपेदे is pass. perf. 3rd per sing of प्र+पद्

Appli:—This refers to persons who are paragons of excellence and hence whose equal cannot be found out.

22. अन्य परिमलः परिमलान्तरम् (कर्म.) अपनीता परिमलान्तरकथा येन-तस्मिन् (बहु.) which does not suffer even the mention of other fragrance. अन्यःपुष्पं पुष्पान्तरम् । देवतरूणां कुसुमे–for देवतरु see Bh. V. I. 19. धन्योऽसि is used ironically here and is equivalent in sense to धिक् त्वाम्. The meaning which is exactly contrary to the meaning of the word is to be indicated by the modulation of voice, this is called काकुः in Sanskrit. Another fine example where this occurs in two places is seen in the opening stanza of the दशरूपक of धनञ्जय, आनन्दनिस्यन्दिषु रूपकेषु व्युत्पत्तिमात्रं फलमल्पबुद्धिः । योऽपीतिहासादिवदाह **साधुस्तस्मै नमः** स्वादुपराङ्मुखाय ॥ (The bold-typed words mean exactly their opposite in sense) The कल्पतरु is the source of the sweetest fragrance and hence the bee is playing a fool in searching for another flower.

Idea:—The bee is a fool if he wants to leave even the flower of the celestial tree.

23. विन्ध्यात् भवति – विन्ध्यभूः having its origin in the mountain विन्ध्य. रथ्यायाः उदकस्य आदानं Receiving the water on the road. शुष्यन्ती–pres. parti. fem. of शुष्, getting dried up. चिराय for a long time.

Idea:—O river don't take street-water.

Appli:—It is not indeed proper for highly dignified persons to stoop to low means even in their adversity.

24. पत्राणां फलानां पुष्पाणां च लक्ष्म्या by the beauty of

leaves, fruits and flowers. "शृकोऽस्त्री श्लक्ष्णतीक्ष्णाग्रे" शूकः – a thorn. उप + सृप् to approach.

Idea:—O बर्बुर, what is there in you to attract us. ?

Appli:—This applies to a wicked man who has nothing attractive, but much that is repulsive.

25. "गहनं काननं वनम्" गहन–forest. कलं-a sweet note. समाना जातिः यस्य तस्य भावः–belonging to the same species; hence साजात्यशङ्कया-mistaking you for one of their own species. निर्गता दया येभ्यः ते निर्दयाः (बहु.) merciless.

Idea :—O कोकिल, do not utter a note, lest you will be killed.

Appil:—where ignorance is bliss, it is folly to be wise. or मूर्खाणां च समाजेषु वरं मौनं हि धीमताम् ॥

26. भवस्य स्त्री भवानी by इन्द्रवरुण &c. (Pan 4–1–49) तरूणां कुलानां (clusters) सुषमां (beauty) अपहरति-सा. जीवानां जातं ष. त. everything that can be classed under the category of जीव. cf. तमध्वरे विश्वजिति क्षितीशं निःशेषविश्राणितकोषजातम् । उपात्तविद्यो गुरुदक्षिणार्थी कौत्सः प्रपेदे वरतन्तुशिष्यः ॥ R. V. 5. 1. "हिमानी हिमसंहतिः" महद् हिमं हिमानी (Pan वार्तिक 4–1–49) Himalaya is always covered with snow–which mars the beauty of the trees. आर्तिः pain–जीवजातस्यार्तिः–-ताम् जनयन्तीं

Idea:—What good, O Himalaya, do you see in the snow that you bear it on your head ?

Appli. This applies to persons who give shelter, for no reason, to people who are a source of constant trouble to society.

27. कलभ-a young elephant–'धूर्वहे धुर्यधौरेयधुरीणाः सधुरंधराः" धुरं वहति सः धुर्यः formed by sutra धुरो यड्ढकौ (Pan. 4–4–77) दानेन सुंदरः (तृ. त.) beautiful on account of ichor. द्वाभ्यां पिबन्ति ते द्विपाः – तेषु धुर्याः best of elephants. शिरसा धार्यः worthy of being borne on the head.

Idea :—O Young elephant, don't disrespect the bee

Appli:—Same as in Bh. V. I–19.

28. विडम्बना–making oneself an object of ridicule. अमराणां (of Gods) तरूणां कुसुमानां सौरभस्य (fragrance) सेवनेन संपूर्णाः (fulfilled) सकलाः कामाः (all desires) यस्य (बहु.) adj. to भ्रमर. for the use of विडम्बना in this sense read, इयं च तेऽन्या पुरतो **विडम्बना** यदूढया वारणराजहार्यया। विलोक्य वृद्धोक्षमधिष्ठितं त्वया महाजनः स्मेरमुखो भविष्यति॥ K. S. 5-70 अन्यत् पुष्पं-पुष्पान्तरम् (कर्म.)

Idea:—The bee is an object of ridicule if he resorts to another flower.

Appli.:—This applies to persons who, although on the pinnacle of prosperity are longing for baser pleasures and thus make themselves objects of ridicule.

29. परैः (काकैः) पुष्टाः—Cuckoos. This is referred to in कालिदास,ऽ शाकुन्तल in the verse प्रागन्तरिक्षगमनात्स्वमपत्य-जातमन्यैर्द्विजैः परभृताः खलु पोषयन्ति (Sak.5–22) उपमा means उपमान-a standard of comparison " उपमोपमानं स्यात् " उपमान is generally superior to उपमेय–the thing that is compared. (in this case आम्र). But here there can be no उपमान found and hence the mango is matchless in its qualities.

Idea:—O माकन्द, the bee did not find your equal.

Appli.:—This applies to some person who is unparalleled in the possession of excellent merits.

30. मालाः करोतीति–a gardener. भीमः भानुः यस्मिन् सः (बहु.) adj. to निदाघ or भीमाः भानवः (the rays) यस्मिन् सः धाराणां आसाराः the showers of rain. भानु – (1) the sun (2) the rays. "निदाघ उष्णोपगमः" निदाघः–the summer. प्रावृषेण्य belonging to the rainy-season, formed irregularly by adding the

termination एण्य by the सूत्र "प्रावृष एण्यः" (Pan 4-3-17) विश्वतः everywhere. विकिरता Instr. 3rd person sing. of the pre. par. of कॄ with वि. व्यरचि pass. aor. 3rd pers. sing. of वि+रच्. पुष्टिः nourishment.

Idea:—The nourishment brought by the water of the gardener cannot be rendered by the amply pouring cloud.

Appli:—Even a little help counts a great deal, when proffered at the opportune moment तदनर्घ्यं यदवसरे दतम्।

31. आरामस्य अधिपतिः the master of the garden. "आरामः स्यादुपवनम्" विवेकेन विकल (तृ. त.) void of thought. रसा–earth. निर्गतः रसः यस्याः सा नीरसा (बहु.) adj. to रसा in which there is no life-giving juice, i. e. barren. परुषीकृताः–च्वि formation-are hardened–वात्याभिः वातसमूहैः by gusts of wind. चण्डः आतपः terrible heat. संहारस्य हेतुः the cause of destruction. धन्वन्–a country without moisture, barren land. "समानौ मरुधन्वानौ ॥ आविस् + कृ to manifest. कुतः अपि from some unknown, unexpected quarter. अमृत water, nectar. vl. धुन्वति for धन्वनि and शकले for सकले. const. चंपकस्य शकले धुन्वति. Not so happy.

Idea:—O cloud, you have manifested yourself unexpectedly.

Appli. This refers to a person whose very life is endangered owing to the presence of various fatal causes when suddenly a succour is sent by God.

32. Vl. स्खलन्मुक्ताभारे भवति परलोकं गतवति (सति) अतिभयेन भ्रान्तानि नयनानि येषां ते (बहु.) with their eyes tremulous owing to excessive fear. गलद् दानं–तस्य उद्रेकः (अतिशयः) तेन भ्रमन्तः अलिकदम्बाः (समूहाः) येषु ते (बहु.) with multitudes of bees hovering around owing to the excess of trickling ichor.

परलोकं गम् – to die. शिव शिव alas ! स्थेमानं धा to stand steadily. लुठन्तः मुक्ताभाराः यस्मिन् तत् (बहु.) adj. to द्वारम् with myriads of pearls from the temples of the slain elephants rolling here and there. This is referred to in परं तुषारस्रुति धौतरक्तं यस्मिन्नदृष्ट्वाऽपि हतद्विपानाम् । विदन्ति मार्गं नखरन्ध्रमुक्तैर्मुक्ताफलैः केसरिणां किराताः । K. S. I. 6. शिवा-a female jackal. v. l. for first line as given above takes it as a loc. absolute when you, who rolled (i.e. caused to roll) multitudes of pearls, have gone to the other world. For भ्रान्तनयनाः the v. l. is भ्रान्तहृदया : which does not make much change.

Idea :—Now female jackals are howling where formerly even big elephants dared not stand.

Appli. A place which people are afraid of approaching when the master is living, becomes condemned after the owner breathes his last.

33. समभावेन doing equal justice to all विपुलां करुणां न अकृत Did not show ample pity towards it, i. e. did not take special notice of it. द्राक्—immediately (adv.) "द्राङ्मंक्षुसपदिद्रुतम्" द्राक् उद्यन्तः कुसुमनिकराः (collection of flowers) तेषाम् । दिशां अन्ताः (ष. त.). मधुपानां कुलानां (clusters of bees) झंकारेण भरितान् filled with the buzzing of bees.) आतेने-Rendered. Perhaps a contrast is intended by the poet between the words तरु & बाल बकुल, तरु meaning a big extensive tree. v. l. विपुलं to be taken with प्रेमाणं but this does not seem happy.

Idea—though neglected by the gardener, the बकुल plant rendered all directions fragrant.

Appli. One who is many times neglected as insignificant, rises to an incredible prominence by his unique intrinsic qualities.

35. बन्धनैः दृढम् strong owing to the roots. मांसलाः strong. दुःखेन गम्यते इति दुर्गः–मह्यः धरः महीधरः a mountain, which is hard to ascend—ज्वालानां आलयः collections of flames. ताभिः वलयीभवन् forming into circles. आधिः एव ज्वरः fever in the form of mental agony. नास्ति करुणा यस्मिन् सः—void of mercy. घस्मरः voracious "भक्षको घस्मरोऽद्मरः" मनाक् a little. "किञ्चिदीषन्मनाक् अल्पे" शतं is an उपलक्षण & means "many"

Idea. O tree you are all safe, excepting from the voracious forest—conflagration

Appli. Even the strongest have to be afraid of something, that will cause their destruction.

35. भीष्मतरैः Comparative of भीष्म terrible. दिनं करोति इ ते दिनकृत् the sun. द्राघीयस is the comparative of दीर्घ. वासरान् days. कथमपि–कथं with चन्, चित् and अपि means "with great difficulty". Compare तस्य स्थित्वा कथमपि पुरः कौतुकाधानहेतोः (etc. Megh. 3) लोचनयोः गोचरः visible by the eyes करकाणां निपातनं shower of hailstones. "वर्षोपलस्तु करका". सा एव कृपा–here used ironically means cruelly. It is the convention of Sanskrit poets that the चातक longs for rain drops, of the स्वाती constellation. cf. कोऽप्याग्रहो गुरुरयं बत चातकस्य पौरन्दरीं यदभिवाच्छति वारिधाराम् The propriety of द्राघीयसः lies in the fact that the days are longest in summer.

Idea—O cloud when should we complain, if you now shower hail—stones upon the चातक ?

Appli. If that very person from whom we expect protection turns against us, where shall we seek for safety ?

36. दवः दहनः forest–conflagration "दवदावौ वनारण्यवह्नी" दवदहनस्य जटालाः ज्वालाः–तेषां जालेन आहतानां भूरुहाणाम्–of trees which are besieged by the cluster of accumulated

flames of the forest-conflagration. भुवि रोहन्ति भूरुहा: trees. परिगलिता: लता: येभ्य: तेषाम् with creepers dropped down. Here is the genitive absolute construction. vide Apte's Guide Sec. 122, also षष्ठी चानादरे (Pan. 2-3-34) cf. नन्दा: पर्यायभूता: पशव इव हता: पश्यतो राक्षसस्य (मुद्रा. 3-27) शैलानां श्रेणीनां शृङ्गेषु on the peaks of the rows of mountains, where rain is not so vitally needed. वि+तॄ to impart, although used in the sense of संप्रदान is sometimes used with the loc. cf. वितरति गुरु: प्राज्ञे विद्यां यथैव तथा जडे etc. (Uttara. 2-4). श्रिय: मद: the pride of wealth in the form of the abundance of water.

Idea:—Improper indeed is the pride of the cloud in pouring rain on the mountain summits neglecting the trees parched in the conflagration.

Appli:—This refers to persons offering abundantly to the already rich, neglecting those who badly want it.

37. पुर: in front of. हन्त alas ! "हन्त हर्षेऽनुकम्पायां वाक्यारम्भविषादयो:" परुषं च तत् गर्जितं च harsh thundering. विह्वलं मन: यस्य स: विह्वलमना: grieved at heart, विश्वस्य आर्ति: तस्या: वारणं-तस्मिन् समर्पितं जीवनं येन who has devoted his life (water-here) in removing the distress of the universe. किमु is used in the sense of doubt or uncertainty; vide Apte's Guide sec. 267 obs. अम्बुन: वाह: the vehicle of water i. e. cloud.

Idea:—O traveller, don't grieve at the thundering, it is merely a cloud, remover of all distresses.

Appli.:—This refers to a person whose harsh external bears behind it, an excessively sympathetic heart.

38. सौरभ्यं fragrance. भुवनानां त्रयम् the triad of worlds. शैत्यं coldness. लोकेभ्य:उत्तरम्–uncommon.

दिशःएव अङ्गनाः तेषां अङ्गणं गता reached the courtyard of the ladies in the form of quarters. निगिरति=निगिलति swallows completely. श्रीखण्ड–a sandal tree. गरलस्य ज्वाला the flame of poison. द्विजिह्वानां आवलिः the line of serpents.

Idea:—O sandal, you have all possible lofty merits but only one drawback that nullifies them all.

Appli.:—This refers to a person who is useless owing to one fault, inspite of his possessing hundreds of merits.

39. अपेक्षा expectation of reciprocal kindness. दाक्षिण्यं–courtesy–politeness. सङ्गतिः a sense of duty to a companion formed through long acquaintance. उन्नत–(1) High up in the sky (2) Noble–minded, magnanimous. Like this cloud, the magnanimous person also removes the pains of the people, irrespective of a return and unimpelled by any other motives like love, courtesy etc.

Appli:—This points to the disinterestedly obliging nature of the magnanimous souls.

40. अम्बुनः जायते इति lotus–born of water. Each of the several qualities described above heighten the value of a lotus. निवासः the abode of लक्ष्मी because she is known as पद्मालया v. l. विलासः--विलासस्थानम् a place of enjoyment. सुराणां हृदयानि हरति इति that which captivates the minds of Gods द्विजेषु उत्तंसः the best or the ornament of the birds i. e हंस. रतिः-–liking.

Idea:—The lotus will reach an extremely high position if it remains attached to the swan.

Appli:—The greatness of great men is greatly enhanced when they cherish love for the best of persons.

41. ग्राव्णां गणा:—तै: with multitudes of stones. साकम्-with. अर्कबिंबं उपमा (उपमानं) येषां ते adj. to मणय:-jewels which are as lustrous as the orb of the sun. उन्नते: प्रौढि: the excess of greatness. The अविवेक deserves निन्दा and उन्नते: परा प्रौढि: deserves स्तुति. नारायण: is termed भगवान् i. e. possessed of the great qualities. These are supposed to be six-ऐश्वर्यस्य समग्रस्य वीर्यस्य यशस: श्रिय: । ज्ञानवैराग्ययोश्चैव षण्णां भग इतीरणा ॥ The author says that he is at a loss to make out whether the milk-ocean deserves praise or blame, because the principle of equality that the ocean follows is wrong. The commentator अच्युतराय says " तत्तद्योग्यतातारतम्यं विवेकेनैव " or even as Kalidasa says" " भवन्ति साम्येऽपि निविष्टचेतसां वपुर्विशेषेष्वतिगौरवा: क्रिया: (K.S. 5-31).

Idea:—O milk-ocean, I cannot decide whether to praise you or to blame you.

Appli:—It is not easy to decide whether the actions of great persons are censurable or praise-worthy.

42. अर्णव-the sea. किम्-what is the use of ? अभ्रमिवाचरति अभ्रायति the past passive participle is अभ्रायित formed from the denominative verb from अभ्र by the sutra उपमानादाचारे (Pan 3-1-10) The body of the sea acts like the sky inasmuch-as it extends over a long distance and possesses blue colour "अभ्रं व्योम" पुष्करमंबरम् सलिलं-water.

Idea:—O sea, all your wealth is useless.

Appli:—This refers to a person who is a repository of immense wealth, but does not utilize even a farthing for doing good to others.

43. इयती so much.-संपत्ति here refers to the copiousness of water. अधुना perhaps refers to the rainy-season

when the lake abounds in water. चण्डाः अंशवः (rays) यस्य सः the sun. अङ्गाराणां निकराः collection of burning charcoal. अंगार means the rays which are as scorching as the living coal. कृशीभूतः–च्वि formation–lean–emaciated, the water being dried up by the heat of the sun. अहह-alas! 'अहहेत्यद्भुते खेदे'. ताम्–तृष्णाम्.

Idea:—O lake, whose thirst will you be able to remove when you are dried up ?

Appli:—Charity should be practised while in prosperity, because it is impossible in adversity.

44. रोषं उरीकरोषि &c. if you do not have recourse to anger. What the author means is this "O sea, great as you are, it is unbecoming on your part to accept water that is given to you by those clouds that begged the same water from you. अर्थयते इति अर्थिन्–a beggar–a mendicant.

Idea:—O sea, do not accept water which has been once given in charity by you.

Appli:—This refers to those miserly persons who are not ashamed of accepting what has once been given in charity.

45. वर्षानदि O river in the rainy-season i. e. a rivulet which is so short–lived that it flows only in the rainy–season. जह्नोः जाता–जह्नुजा–जह्नु, the son of king होत्रक, who hid the Ganges under his thigh, finding her troublesome to him. Hence the Ganges is named after him. (vide वा. रा. बालकांड सर्ग 43) The Ganges is decidedly a far greater river in comparsion with the वर्षानदी. स्रोतस् a stream. तरङ्गाणां भङ्गः the dashing or breaking of waves. प्रकटीकृ, च्वि formation, to manifest.

Idea:—O वर्षानदि it is unbecoming for you to mainfest breaking-waves, before the Ganges.

Appli:—It is not proper for an insignificant person to make an ostentatious display of one's pride before the great.

46. पौलोम्याः पत्युः कानने In the garden of the lord of पौलोमी i. e. of Indra. गीर्वाणानां भूमीरुहः the trees of gods i.e. the desire-yielding trees. "गीर्वाणा दानवारयः" for कल्पवृक्ष see note on Bh. V. I. 28. आदौ आघ्रातानि पश्चात् समुज्झितानि first smelt and then given up. निर्गता जरा येभ्यः ते निर्जराः the un-ageing i. e. Gods. मधु एव व्रतं यस्य सः मधुव्रतः the bee. मधुव्रते माध्वीकमाकांक्षति &c. is the loc. absolute construction. विधिवशात् through the force of his ill-luck as he has to resort to an earthly lotus for seeking for honey–he who has once tasted celestial flowers. माध्वीकं–honey. लोभं अंचसि lit. goes to greed i. e. become greedy in giving honey to the bee.

Idea:—O lotus, do not be greedy in giving honey to the bee who has tasted the celestial trees.

Appli:—Same as in Bh. V. I. 19.

47. मृणालानां पटली ष. त. The cluster of lotus fibres. The swans live on the lotus fibres; vide Megh. the latter half of verse 11. नितरां पीतानि drunk to the heart's content. कृतः उपकारः येन सः (बहु) one who has done obligations in return.

Idea:—O swan ! how will you repay the obligation ?

Appli:—This refers to a person who is asked how he would show his gratitude towards one who has conferred upon him a number of obligations.

48. कुसुमानां आकरः (ष. त.) the vernal season. उल्लसन्तीनां मञ्जरीणां पुञ्जे on the cluster of the blooming sprouts. मञ्जुलानि गुञ्जितानि(कर्म.)the sweet hummings रचयन् prducing. उत्सवान् आतनोः enjoyed excessively तान्–refers to the

event of the past. cf. उन्मत्तः स च राजपुत्रनिवहस्ते बन्दिनस्ताः कथाः । सर्वं यस्य वशादगात् स्मृतिपथं कालाय तस्मै नमः ॥ तस्मिन् रसालशाखिनि कृशां दशां अञ्चति (सति) loc. absolute construction, showing time. When that mango-tree is shorn of leaves. दैवात्-through ill-luck. विनय-gratitude, modesty.

Idea:—It is worst meanness, that a bee should show ingratitude towards a leafless mango tree.

Appli:—It is the height of ingratitude to forsake our benefactor who is in adversity, with whom we have passed our best days.

49. कलय Know. कृष्णसार-a black antelope. हरि here means a lion. It is used to mean many more animals. यमानिलेन्द्र चन्द्रार्क विष्णु सिंहांशुवाजिषु । शुकाहि कपिभेकेषु हरिर्ना कपिलेत्रिषु ॥ गर्वेण निमीलिते अक्षिणी येन सः (बहु.) Whose eyes are closed through pride. हरेः विहारस्य वसुंधरा the play-ground of the lion. भिन्नानां करीन्द्राणां कुम्भेभ्यः (गलिताभिः) मुक्ताभिः पूर्णा-Filled with pearls dropping down from the temples of the best of elephants which are torn open. (by the lion) मय is the termination added according to तत्प्रकृत-वचने मयट् (Pan. 5-4-21) in the sense of अधिकरण., "Subsisting therein". मुक्तामयीं full of pearls. एणी female of a कृष्णसार deer.

Idea:—O deer, don't enjoy thoughtlessly, you are in the vicinity of death.

Appli:—A man should not remain immersed in enjoyment, when danger is imminent.

50. जठरे ज्वलनः—The gastric fire तेन ज्वलता adj. to हरिणा अपगता शंका (scruples) यथा स्यात् तथा-unscrupulously. हरिणानां आली a herd of deer.

Idea:—Even though starving, a lion will never attack deer.

Appli:—The great never stoop to base means even in adversity.

51. भिन्नाः करिणां कुम्भाः तेभ्य विस्खलतां मौक्तिकानां आवलिभिः मही अंचिता–The earth is covered with the rows of pearls dropping from the temples of elephants torn open. हरिणानां अन्तिके near the deer.

Idea:—The lion should not speak about his valour to the deer.

Appli:—The great should never speak about their greatness to the insignificant persons.

52. मदेनान्धे ईक्षणे यस्य—Whose eyes are blinded owing to rut. गजानां श्रेणीनां नाथः—the leader of the herds of elephants. जटिल formed by adding the term इलच् (इल) in the sense of censure according to सूत्र (लोमादि पोमादि) पिच्छादिभ्यः शनेलचः (Pan. 5–2–100) (lit–intermixed)– dense. If no censure is implied it assumes the form जटावान्. स्थितिं धा–to stand. कुम्भिनां भ्रांतिः तया–mistaking (the rocks) for elephants. खराश्च ते नखराश्च तैः विद्रावितः महान् गुरूणां ग्राव्णां ग्रामः येन (बहु.) adj. to हरिपतिः–The lion who has torn with his pointed nails a collection of big rocks. " ग्रावाणौ शैलपाषाणौ ".

Idea:—O lord of elephants, the lion is sleeping now, so leave this place if you want to save your life.

Appli:—The weak ones should not stay at all even when their strong enemies are asleep.

53. गजानां राजा गजराजः formed by राजाह: सखिभ्यष्टच् (Pan. 5–4–91) तस्य पोतः the young one of the lord of elephants. "यानपात्रे शिशौ पोतः" गुरुः गर्वः (कर्म.) तेन गुम्फितः तृ. तः Being puffed up with great pride. गिरेगह्वरेषु in the caves of the mountain. स्तनं धयति–Sucking the (mother's) breast. This shows that the cub of the lion is so very

young. हरिशिशुः–The cub of a lion. करेणवः परिशेषिताः यस्यां सा (बहु.) adj. to मही–with only the female elephants remaining. "करेणुरिभ्यां स्त्री" The idea is that the moment the cub of the lion is roused, he will slay all the elephants and only the female ones will be remaining as they are the objects of pity. cf. करिण्यः कारुण्यास्पदं Bh. V. I–1 भविता–भविष्यति. cf. सिंहः शिशुरपि निपतति मदमलिनकपोलभित्तिषु गजेषु ॥

Idea:–The cub of the elephant is asked not to stir about arrogantly lest the cub of the lion might awake.

Appli.:–The fiery, though young, are capable of vanquishing mighty enemies.

54. निसर्गात्–naturally. कृती-well-versed. आरामः–a garden. तरूणां कुलस्य समारोपे सुकृती–ingenious in planting myriads of trees. कोणस्य अन्तरम् (ष. त.) तत्र गतः–planted in some corner. जगतः जालं– the net of the world i. e. the whole world. कुसुमानां भरस्य सौरभ्येण भरितं–filled with the fragrance of the multitude of flowers.

Appli:—The great are sure to shine out though neglected by the thoughtless.

55. राघव is an excessively big fish. परिचलतां कल्लोलानां कोलाहलैः-By the loud uproar of huge waves moving here and there. हरित्सु (तिष्ठन्तः) दन्तावलाः–elephants standing at the quarters. "दिशस्तु ककुभः काष्ठा आशाश्च हरितश्च ताः" There is a mythological reference here to the eight guardian elephants that are supposed to support the earth, they are enumerated in the following verse, ऐरावतः पुण्डरीको वामनः कुमुदोऽञ्जनः। पुष्पदन्तः सार्वभौमः सुप्रतीकश्च दिग्गजाः। They preside respectively over the eight cardinal points. पूर्वाग्नेयी दक्षिणा च नैर्ऋती पश्चिमा तथा। वायवी चोत्तरैशानी दिशा अष्टाविमाः स्मृताः ॥ मन्थाश्चासौ आद्रिश्च, तस्य भ्रमणं तस्य भ्रममापेदिरे–

mistook it (the movement of waters) for the revolving of the mountain that was made to work as the churn. When Gods and demons churned the ocean for getting nectar, they are said to have made the मन्दर mountain the churning handle. हृदि is optional locative sing of हृदय formed according to पद्दन्नोमास् हृद् etc. (Pan. 6-1-63) 'दन्ती दन्तावलो हस्ती ' दन्तावले is formed by the affix वलच् (वल) after दन्त when a name is formed. See Sutra दन्तशिखात् संज्ञायाम (Pan. 5-2-113) and the final of the word दन्त is lengthened according to the Sutra वले (Pan. 6-3-118) तुङ्गश्चासौ तिमिङ्गिलः तस्य अंगस्य कवलीकारः (the action of swallowing) एव क्रिया तस्यां कोविदः । " सन्सुधीः कोविदो बुधः ',-An expert in the work of swallowing the body of a lofty तिमिङ्गिल fish. तिमि-तिमिङ्गिल-तिमिङ्गिलगिल and राघव is the order, the succeeding one swallowing the preceding one. कवल-a mouthful. Hence कवलीकृ-to swallow. " क्रोडं भुजान्तरम् " (bosom). द्रवक्केलिपरिहासाः क्रीडा खेला च नर्म च । केलि (संबन्धी) कलहः तेन त्यक्तः अर्णवः येन सः-who quitted the sea due to the quarrel in sport.

Idea:—where will a राघव fish-whose movements strike terror in the heart of smaller fish, play ?

Appli:—If every-day actions of great persons strike terror in the hearts of the smaller ones, while in their homes, where are they to go then ?

56. " मतङ्गजो गजो नागः " मत्तैः मतङ्गजैः लूनं broken by intoxicated elephants. तुषारेण आर्दिताः तैः-Afflicted by frost. " तुषारस्तुहिनं हिमं " ग्रीष्मजस्य भीष्मस्य भानोः किरणैः-by the rays of the terrible summer sun " दारुणं भीषणं भीष्मं " भस्मीकृ-to reduce to ashes, कोणं गता (द्वि. त.) lying in the corner. मुहुः-frequently. " मुहुः पुनः पुनः शश्वदभीक्ष्णमसकृत् समाः " लवङ्गस्य लतिका-The clove plant.

Idea:—when the whole forest is destroyed the poor tender clove plant also has to yield to destruction.

Appli:—when the very master, who is resorted to, meets with destruction, the servants also who seek his shelter must naturally die along with him.

57. स्वर्लोक: स्वर्लोक:-सुप्सुपूमसमास: स्वर्लोकस्य शिखायां मणि: The crest jewel of the celestial world. सुराणां तरूणां ग्रामस्य धाम—The abode of the collections (ग्राम) of the celestial trees. " वृन्देऽपि ग्राम: " पौलोमीपुरुहूतयो: " पुरुहूत: पुरन्दर: " पौलोमी–इन्द्राणी (पुलोम्न: अपत्यं स्त्री) पुलोमन् was the name of a demon. पुण्यानां आवलि:—a series of merits or meritorious acts. परिणति:—a noun from परि+नम्–fulfilment. नन्दन is the name of the garden of इन्द्र " इय उच्चैश्रवा:, सूतो मातलि:, नन्दनं वनम् " खाण्डवरङ्गताण्डवनट: "ताण्डवं नटनं नाट्यं लास्यं नृत्यं च नर्तने" खाण्डवं एव रङ्ग: तत्र ताण्डवं तस्मिन् नट:—The actor, dancing on the stage in the form of the खाण्डव forest. खाण्डव The name of a forest in कुरुक्षेत्र, dear to Indra and burnt by अग्नि with the assistance of अर्जुन and कृष्ण. रङ्ग:–a stage. " रङ्गो नृत्यरणक्षितौ " इति मेदिनी. " अग्निर्वैश्वानरो वह्नि: " वैश्वानर:–विश्वे नरा: अस्य इति विश्वानर:–विश्वानरस्य अपत्यं वैश्वानर:—God fire. (Pan 4–1–114).

Idea :—Although the celestial garden (नन्दन) is great in many respects yet it has dread from fire.

Appli:—Although a person may be inconceivably great yet there does exist dread for him from some quarter at least.

54. स्वस्यां स्वस्यां व्यापृतौ (occupation) मग्नं मानसं येषां ते- तेषां भाव: तया–Because there mind would be engaged in their respective occupation. चञ्च्वा: कोटिना विपाटितं अररस्य पुटं येन स.–one who has broken open the panes of a door (of the cage) with the point of the beak. "कपाटमररं तुल्ये"

मनोरथमयं पीयूषं=" पीयूषममृतं सुधा " –nectar in the form of the desire. वारणस्य करस्य इव आकारः यस्य सः बहु.–having the form of the trunk of an elephant, " करो वर्षोपले रश्मौ पाणौ प्रत्यायशुण्डयोः । इति मेदिनी. फणिषु ग्रामणीः–the best of serpents. " ग्रामणीर्नापिते पुंसि श्रेष्ठे " ग्रामं नयति—उ. त. Leader of men.

Idea:—While the parrot is planning his escape from the cage, the unforeseen peril of the serpent creeps in.

Appli:—Man proposes but God disposes or " मनसा चिन्तितं कार्यं दैवमन्यत्र चिन्तयेत् । "

59. चाञ्चल्यं जुषन्ते इति चाञ्चल्यजुषः (उ. त.) Those who like fickleness (i. e. those who cannot remain steady.) श्रिताः नगाः यैः ते (बहु.)–who are residing in mountains. कल्लोलानां मालाभिः आकुलाः (तृ. त.)–Agitated by lines of surging waves. अंबुधेः कामिनी–A river. गाह् 1 A. to bathe in. The verb implying motion governs the acc. or the dat. of the place to which the motion is directed. " गत्यर्थकर्मणि द्वितीयाचतुर्थ्यौ चेष्टायामनध्वनि " (Pan. 2–3–12,) व्यवसित is the p. p. p. of वि + अव् + सो (4 P.) यद् means ' since ' in as much as उच्छलतः अम्बुनः निर्भरेण महद्भिरावर्तैः (स्यादावर्तोऽम्भसां भ्रमः) समावर्तितः–tossed by the great whirlpools of surging volume of waters. गजेषु ग्रामणीः (स. त.) the best of elephants. रसायाः तलं–the bottom of the earth. ' ग्रावाणौ शैलपाषाणौ. '

Idea:—O deer, do not venture to bathe in the surging river in which even an elephant has been drowned.

Appli:—Why should pigmies try to achieve that in accomplishing which even persons of strength have met with destruction.

60. पोतः–child. 'यानपात्रे शिशौ पोतः'–मद. (युक्तः) दन्तावलः

तस्य धी: तया–thinking it to be an elephant in rut. हरितां अन्ताः (ष. त.) ends of quarters. किम् Joined with इति has the sense of " why " cf. किमित्यपास्याभरणानि यौवने धृतं त्वया वार्धकशोभि वल्कलम् । K. S. 5–44. दृशः अन्ता. ष. त. side-glances. नवश्चासौ नीलश्च–new and dark. जलस्य धरः (ष. त.) the holder of water (cloud).

Idea : O cub, do not cast angry side-glances at the thundering of the cloud, mistaking it for an elephant in rut.

61. नीरं ददाति (उ. त.) a cloud. अलं " enough " governs the instru. cf. अलं महीपाल तव श्रमेण प्रयुक्तमप्यस्त्रमितो वृथा स्यात् । न पादपोन्मूलनशक्ति रंहः शिलोच्चये मूर्च्छति मारुतस्य । R. V. 34 and the Sutra पर्याप्तिवचनेष्वलमर्थेषु (Pan. 3-4-66) धीराश्च ते ध्वनयः (कर्म.) तैः—धीरध्वनिभिः with sonorous rumblings. मासिकः–"मासमात्रकालिकः" one month old. उन्मदः च असौ वारणः च तस्य बुद्धया–thinking it to be an intoxicated elephant. जठरस्य मध्ये–मध्येजठरम्—अव्य. acc. to Pan. पारे मध्ये षष्ठया वा (Pan. 2–1–18).

Idea : Even the foetus of the lioness, one month old, is moving at the thundering.

Appli. तेजसां हि न वयः समीक्ष्यते । R. V. 11–1 or तेजसा सह जातानां वयः कुत्रोपयुज्यते । Heroism depends upon pre-natal impressions and not on age.

62. वेतण्डानां (गजानां) गंडानां कंडूत्यां पांडित्यं–तस्य परिपंथी–तेन being the obstacle in the skill of the rubbing of the temples by the elephants. परिपन्थी an obstacle " अरातिप्रत्यर्थिपरिपन्थिनः " cf. अकरिष्यदसौ पापमतिनिष्करुणैव सा । नाभविष्यमहं तत्र यदि तत्परिपन्थिनी ॥ Malt. 9–51.

Idea:—The same as in the 51st verse.

Appli:—Timid persons do not deserve the heroic exploits of the brave to be related to them.

63. " जनुर्जननजन्मानि जनिरुत्पत्तिरुद्भवः " निर्मलतः=निर्मलात् It is born of clear water. 'वामा वनिता महिला तथा' वामायाः मुखेन स्पर्धते इति–competing with the face of the woman. The word वामा does not mean an ordinary woman here but a woman with bewitching beauty. Bhanuji Dixit, the commentator on Amarkosha derives this as वमति स्नेहम् i. e. that which exhibits love and as such becomes an object of reciprocal affection. It is customary with the poets to utilize the lotus as the standard of comparison. Vide चकितहरिणलोललोचनायाः क्रुधि तरुणारुणतारहारिकान्ति । सरसिजमिदमाननं च तस्याः सममिति चेतसि संमदं विधत्ते ॥ K. P. 10–2 गीर्वाणानां चेतः हरति इति (उप०) that which captivates the minds of Gods. " गीर्वाणा दानवारयः " The lotus is indispensable for the speech of the great poets; for it is frequently used as a standard of comparison and the cupid cannot do anything without a lotus because it is his arrow. See अरविन्दमशोकं etc. Cupid is shown as boasting of the prowess of these arrows of his, which in his opinion are more potent than even thunderbolt of Indra. प्रसीद विश्राम्यतु वीर वज्रं शरैर्मदीयैः कतमः सुरारिः । बिभेतु मोघीकृतबाहुवीर्यः स्त्रीभ्योपि कोपस्फुरिताधराभ्यः । K. S. 3–9 and hence जगन्नाथपण्डित calls अरविन्द to be the सर्वस्व of काम. मधुप- (1) a bee (2) a drunkard.

Idea:—A lotus–repository of all greatness, containing a feeling of love for a bee–is condemnable.

Appli:—It is a stain on the character of a person endowed with supernatural qualifications to entertain love for mean minded persons.

64. लीलायां मुकुलिते नयने यथा स्याताम् तथा (अव्ययी०) with your eyes half closed in amorous sport. लीला is an amorous sport. ' हेला लीलेत्यमी हावाः क्रियाः शृङ्गारभावजाः ' । सुखं

स्वपनं-sleeping at ease. परिणामे विषम: हरि:-the lion who is terrible in the end. (result.) (i. e. entering into enmity with this lion will lead to a grave catastrophe.

Idea:—O elephant, do not be engrossed in sport. You are thereby aggravating the enmity with the lion.

Appli:—Treating the mighty lightly kindles their wrath.

65. द्वौ रदौ येषां ते-तेषाम् elephants. " द्विरदोऽनेकपो द्विप: " पराञ्चन्ति from परा + अञ्-are withdrawn, are taken back.

Idea:—" मकृज्जल्पन्ति पण्डिता: " The wise keep their own counsel.

66. " संभूति: noun from सं + भू birth. दातॄणां गुरु:-तस्य the preceptor i. e. best of donors. लोकेषु उत्तरा:-Extraordinary. अर्थिषु प्रवरा: तेषां यदर्थितं तस्य अर्पणविधौ. In the act of granting the solicitations of the best of solicitors. v. l. अर्थिप्रकरार्थतर्पणविधौ—In the act of satisfying the desires of the multitude of supplicants. (अर्थिनां प्रकर:-तस्य अर्था:-तेषां तर्पणविधौ).

Idea:—Had the celestial tree been discriminate in granting the requests of the supplicants, all its merits would have been extraordinary.

Appli:—Sometimes persons, possessed of a number of extraordinary merits, have one serious defect.

67. अपगता घृणा यस्मात्-स:-relentless. अनुताप:-remorse. मा (स्म) कृथा: imperative sense of the aorist; see note on the verse Bh. V. 1-6. विमलानि च तानि क्षेत्राणि (कर्म०) तेषु-In sacred places. गूढ: आशय: येषां ते-whose motives are concealed i e. hypocrites. " अभिप्रायश्छन्द आशय: " इति व

वसन्ति–सहस्रश एव वसन्ति। त्वया तुल्या कक्षा (गणना or अवस्था) येषां ते-whose state resembles yours or who are considered similar to you (in point of wickedness). कक्षा–गूढ–हिंसनादिकल्पना इति अच्युतरायाः.

Idea:—The fowler is asked not to feel remorse at heart as there are thousands of wicked persons like him.

Appli:—Here the poet intends to bring to light the secret hypocritical nature of the courtiers and so-called holy persons in holy places. In his opinion they resemble the fowler who slays those creatures that confide in him.

68. विश्वास्य–Gerund of the causal of श्वस् with वि–Having inspired confidence in. काश्यपि–O earth. " क्षोणिर्ज्या काश्यपी क्षितिः " कश्यपस्य इयं–she ought to be discriminate as she is related to the great sage.

Idea:—Even the earth has lost discretion hence she gives a resort to the cheaters.

Appli:—the same as that of the verse 13 in this Vilasa.

69. जगद्धितमयी–beneficial to the world. अन्या has a typical meaning–extra-ordinary. आर्याणां हृद्या—captivating the noble. v.l. आर्तहृद्या–captivating the hearts of the distressed. " हृदि स्पृश्यते मनोज्ञत्वात् " दवीयः–comparative from दूर.

Idea: Everything belonging to the learned beggars description.

70. आपदं गतः – द्वि. त.–fallen into adversity. महान् आशयः येषां ते महाशयाः (बहु.) तेषां चक्रे वर्तते इति–the foremost of the high-souled or magnanimous. विस्तारयति-extends-causal of स्तृ with वि. पूर्वं अकृतं–अकृतपूर्वं–not shown (lit. done) before.

उदार: भाव:-तम्-generosity-broadmindedness. कालागुरु:-a kind of sandal.

Idea: Sandal when cast into fire emits greater fragrance.

Appli: The great shine the more luxuriantly in adversity.

cf. कर्पूर: पावकस्पृष्टः सौरभं लभतेतराम् ॥

71. विश्वस्य अभिरामा: गुणा:, तेषां गौरवेण गुम्फिता: (तृ. त.) तेषां adj. to निर्मलधियाम्–Filled with abundance (गौरव) of qualities agreeable to the whole world. निर्मला धी: येषां ते (बहु.)–Those whose minds are pure i.e. free from jealousy etc. लोकं पृणन्ति ते (द्वि. अलुक्) adj. to परिमल–The fragrance that brings satisfaction to the people. काश्मीरदेशे जायते–saffron is so called because it is produced in काश्मीर, नितान्तं रम्यां–excessively pleasing.

Idea : Saffron though bitter is very agreeable.

Application : Even the wrath of persons who are selfless is pleasing. cf. रोषोऽपि निर्मलधियां रमणीय एव् ।

Compare:—ये ये हताश्चक्रधरेण राजंस्त्रैलोक्यनाथेन जनार्दनेन ।
ते ते गता विष्णुपुरीं प्रयाता: क्रोधोऽपि देवस्य वरेण तुल्य: ॥
पांडवगीता.

72. लीलया लुण्ठित: शारदाया: पुरस्य महत्या: संपद: भर: यै: तेषाम् (बहु,)–who in (mere) sport have plundered the excess of great wealth in the city of शारदा—the goddess of learning. विद्याया: सद्मन: विनिर्गलत· कणान् मुष्णन्ति ते—adj. to पामरा:—those who steal (of course hence very little of) particles dripping from the house of knowledge. " विवर्ण: पामरो नीच:"–an insignificant person. अद्य वा श्वो वा इति अद्यश्व: सुप्सुप् समास to–day or tomorrow. v.l.–अद्यश्वा: It is explained as अद्य वर्तमानदिने श्वयन्ते वर्धन्ते which means very recently born and is to be taken with शकुन्तशिशव:, शशा:

and शालावृकाः. मूर्ध्नि पदं धा-lit. to place a foot on the head i.e. to disparage, to defeat, to subdue, to overpower. " कुण्डली गूढपाद् चक्षुश्रवाः काकोदरः फणी" फणी–One possessing a hood. ' शालावृकाःकपिक्रोष्टुश्वानः " Here it is better to take क्रोष्टु leaving the other two meanings.

Idea : If persons with little knowledge were to prattle before the wise, impossible things will occur.

73. गुरूणाम्–of great persons. " गुरुस्तु गीष्पतौ श्रेष्ठे गुरौ पितरि दुर्भरे. " परुषाणि अक्षराणि यासु-adj. to गीर्भिः containing harsh (words) letters. महत्त्वं यान्ति Attain greatness. न लब्धानि शाणे उत्कषणानि यैस्ते (बहु.) adj. to मणयः–That have not undergone the scratching on the touchstone ' चूडा किरीटं केशाश्च संयता मौलयस्त्रयः ' । मौलिः-the head. ' कदाचिज्जातु. '

Idea:—Unless privations at the hands of great persons are put up with, none should hope to achieve greatness. cf. Marathi टांकीचे घाव सोसल्यावांचून दगडाला देवपण येत नाहीं.

75. क्षितेः इन्द्राः (तत्पु०) Lords of the earth. ' पिशुनौ खलसूचकौ ' पिशुनः जनः (कर्म०) a wicked man. विषस्य धरः–a repository of venom–a snake. मसीपटलं (षी) (षि) (सि)-the coat of soot. विधुः-the moon. ' विधुर्विष्णौचन्द्रमसि ' " भजतेतराम्–अत्यन्तं सेवते." तराम् is affixed to the verb in order to express the comparative degree. The verse perhaps brings to the world's notice that not only the earthly things like पटीरजन्मा or दीप but even celestial things like the moon, imitate the actions of the king, and hence the necessity of the king's character being a pattern of good conduct.

75. " पुरुषाः पूरुषा नराः " हितैः आचरणैः-by charitable conduct (कर्म०). अमन्दं adv. without growing dull i. e. incessantly "उदारो दातृमहतोः". Here उदार means "generous"

(in giving pleasure to the clusters of कैरविणीs) कैरव is a night lotus described as white in colour and blooming at the appearance of the moon. " सिते (कमले) कुमुदकैरवे ".

Idea:—The good by their very nature are engaged in the work of doing good to others. cf. प्रकृतिरियं विमलानां क्लिश्यन्ति यदन्यकार्येषु ।

76. महान् चासौ उपकार: च-great obligation. निर्गत: आतङ्क: यस्मात् स: निरातङ्क:-fearless. " रुक्तापशङ्कास्वातङ्क:" पीत्वा (1) Having drunk (milk) (2) Having swallowed i. e. forgotten (the obligation.) प्रत्युत-on the contrary. अपि is sometimes replaced by प्रत्युत. cf. अयं वत्सो न केवलं ध्रियते प्रत्युत प्राञ्जलिना गरुडेन पर्युपास्यमानस्तिष्ठति: (Nag 5) " काकोदर: फणी ". समानं उदरं यस्य स:-सोदर:-a brother. काकोदरस्य सोदर:- the brother of a serpent.

Idea:—A wicked man is as ungrateful as a serpent who bits the person who nourishes him with milk.

77. पांडित्यं परिहृत्य—Setting aside cleverness-learnedness. बंदित्वं—the duty of a bard or panegyrist. " बन्दिन: स्तुतिपाठका: " दु:खेन प्राप्यते-दुष्प्रापं-difficult to be obtained, unobtainable. The idea in the first line is, for whom flattery has been resorted to, after setting aside love for lore and truth. तत्र रूढ:-when he is established there-firmly-rooted there. निगीर्य has the same force as पीत्वा in the preceding verse. पूर्वेषां उपकाराणां आवलिं-series of previous obligations. प्रत्यवतिष्ठते-स्था with प्रति and अव-(" stand as an obstacle ") becomes Atm. समवप्रविभ्य: स्थ: (Pan. 1-3-22.)

Idea:—" पय:पानं भुजङ्गानां केवलं विषवर्धनम् "-Obligations shown to a wicked fellow result in ingratitude.

78. अपायं शङ्कन्ते इति-Those who suspect harm. कापट्ये एव दोष:—The defect of fraud. This तृतीया here shows

हेतुः. दूरेण is used adverbially at a distance. "आशीविषो विषधरः "-serpent-" आश्यां (दंष्ट्रायां) विषं अस्य ". विसृज्-to abandon, to leave.

Idea:—Those shrewd persons who apprehend fear from the deceitful, give no chance to them even to approach them.

79. आसङ्गः-आसक्तिः-Attachment, विशेषः आसङ्गः व्यासङ्गः-परस्य अर्थे व्यासङ्गः (तत्पु.)-Extreme attachment for doing good to others. स्वार्थः एव परः यस्य सः (बहु.) तत्ता स्वार्थपरता-selfishness. उपजहत् is the nom. sing. of the present participle of उप + हा. The ending त् is not changed to न (vide rule 23 lesson 16-Bhandarkar's second book of sanskrit). गुणभूतेषु-between the three gunas-सत्व, रजस् and तमस् and beings. (भूतs). v. 1 गुरुभूतेषु-गुरु is an adv. अभेद-(जातं) एकत्वम्-(शाकपार्थिवादिः). अन्तः is an adverb-in the interior. ललितश्चोदात्तश्च महिमा (कर्म॰)-the beautiful and generous greatness. स्फुरति lit. throbs, manifests itself voluntarily. " समर्थस्त्रिषु शक्तिस्थे " समर्थः-powerful. कोऽपि.-indescribable. cf. तत्तस्य किमपि द्रव्यं यो हि यस्य प्रियो जनः। जयतितराम्-comparative from जयति.

Idea:—The man who is void of partiality and benevolent is the one who is victorious.

cf. अयं निजः परो वेति गणना लघुचेतसाम् ।
उदारचरितानां तु वसुधैव कुटुम्बकम् ॥

There is another interpretation also that has been given in many commentaries, which pertains to grammar. The कोऽपि पुरुषः in the last line refers to the तत्पुरुष समास to which all the adjectives mentioned in in the verse apply. (1) परार्थव्यासङ्गात्स्वार्थ परतां उपजहत. It abandons the meaning of itself (स्वस्य: अर्थः) by its attachment to the other meaning (परार्थे). In a तत्पुरुष compound the two members give up their individual meaning and form some different meaning. e. g. in the compound. राज्ञः पुरुषः, the whole compound राजपुरुष points to a meaning different from that denoted either by राजन् or पुरुष taken individually. Thus the first line can be applied to the तत्पुरुष compound. There is अभेदैकत्व i. e. unity born from non-difference between the two members which are the components (गुणभूत) whereas the compound is the गुणी or the whole. Before the formation of the तत्पुरुष compound there is भेद between the two members but after the compound is formed there is absolute unity in the meaning. The third adjective is स्वभावाद्यस्यान्तः सकलोदात्त-महिमा स्फुरति. सकलोदात्तमहिमा is adj. to अन्तः-सकलः उदात्तस्य महिमा यस्मिन्-with all glory of an उदात्त accent; The अन्त of a तत्पुरुष compound possesses all the greatnees of an उदात्त accent, whose end by its very nature throbs, whose last syllable (अंतः) is always उदात्त. According to vedic grammar the last letter of a Tatpurusha compound is always accented or उदात्त. That तत्पुरुष is always able i. e. the words in the compound are capable of forming a समास i. e. they are capable of always giving one connected meaning.

This twisted sense shows too much mania for puns. Thus the natural beauty of a poem is marred, it becomes dull, insipid and artificial. मंगट also voices the same opinion when he says " शब्दचित्रं वाच्यचित्रमव्यङ्ग्यं त्ववरं स्मृतम् " K. P. 1-5.

80. " द्वौ वंशौ कुलमस्करौ " वंशः-Bamboo, गुण-a rope-a quality. सङ्गविशेष in the case of पुरुष means " good company ", in the other case it means " being fixed

to." "तुम्बीफलेन विकल: (त.)-void of a तुम्बी fruit. वंशभव: and गुणवान् are to be construed both with पुरुष and वीणादण्ड:. In the first instance वंशभव will mean "born of a noble family," in the second, "born of a bamboo." गुणवान् in the first case means "possessed of good qualities" in the second "possessed of strings."

Idea :—Inspite of the possession of a number of noble qualities, men are valued from the company they keep.

81. निखिलेषु रसायनेषु महित: (स. त.)-रसायन is the elixir of life. It is a medicine that prolongs life and prevents old age, similar to अमृत. महित:-honoured, prominent. The धन्वन्तरीय निघण्टु in the 4th (करवीरादि) वर्ग enumerates the qualities of this कन्दलशुन. The various names that have been given there show its unique position in the sphere of medicine. रसोनो लशुनो ऽरिष्टो म्लेच्छकन्दो महौषधम्। महाकन्दो रसोन: etc. The peculiar qualities are स्वादुरसो ऽतिबल्य:। वृष्यश्चमेधा-स्वरवर्णचक्षुर्भग्नास्थिसन्धानकर: सुतीक्ष्ण:—pungent excessively–It gives great strength and vitality, it is used in joining fractures, developes memory, sweetens voice, improves the colour of the body and gives a cooling sensation and improves the eye-sight. It is called रसोन because it contains all the five main tastes (रसऽ) with the exception of अम्ल (sour). अमिता: गुणा: यस्मिन् स: (बहु.) possessed of innumerable qualities.

82. सन्त: गुणा: यस्य (बहु.) One possessed excellent qualities. विपदम् गत: (द्वि. त.) reduced to adversity. मूर्च्छां गत:–fallen in swoon. The मूर्च्छा and मरण are to be construed with पारद also. It cannot be utilized unless it is संस्कृत i.e. operated upon. राजनिघण्टु in (सुवर्णादि) 6th वर्ग mentions–संस्कारहीनं खलु सूतराजं (पारदं) सेवेत यस्तस्य करोति

बाधाम् । देहस्य नाशं विदधाति नूनं कुष्ठादिदोषान् जनयेन्नराणाम्–when मूर्च्छित it removes all diseases (मूर्च्छित–मूर्च्छितो हरते व्याधीन्) if मारित–it gives all Siddhis (सर्वां सिद्धिकरो लीनः , it achieves all objects. मूर्च्छना and मारण are two chemical processes of treating quick-silver corresponding to calcination and purification respectively. The two processes of मूर्च्छना and मारण have been explained in detail in the शार्ङ्गधरसंहिता मध्यमखंड अध्याय १२ verses 4 to 12 and 35–37 and we leave the critical study of these verses for students more particularly interested in that science.

83. वनस्य अन्तः (ष. त.) the boundary or skirts of a forest. (Here it is उपवन). खेलन्ती–Present Participle femin. of खेल्. शशकस्य शिशुः (त.) a young hare. चकिता–विस्मिता startled. सपदि immediately " सद्यः सपदि तत्क्षणे ". भयस्य हर्ता–भयहर्ता (त०) the remover of danger. भुजयोः प्रान्तः The space between the two hands (bosom) i.e. embraces her husband through fear. दश वदनानि यस्य सः–तेन नीता (त०) The ten faced i.e. Ravan. हलानि इव रदाः येषां ते (ब०)–whose teeth were as big as ploughs. परि+इ to surround-परीता surrounded. विवशा-विगतः वशः (control) यस्याः सा–helpless. कामपि दशाम् to an indescribably (pitiable) plight.

Idea:—सुखात्तु यो याति नरो दरिद्रतां धृतः शरीरेण मृतः स जीवति । (मृच्छ. 1-10.) The only difference between the two is that the result of adversity succeeding prosperity is expressed in the quotation, whereas in the verse under consideration it is suggested by the words कामपि etc.

84. "गीर्वाणा दानवारयः" गीर्वाणाः-Gods. पुरः governs the gen. of that with reference to which the direction is shown (vide Apte's guide sec. 112.) cf. तिष्ठन् भाति पितुः पुरो भुवि यथा (Nag. 1–6). निजभुजबलस्य आहोपुरुषिकां self-

conceitedness of strength of one's own arms. अहं पुरुषः इत्यहंकारवान् अहोपुरुषः-तस्य भावः आहोपुरुषिका-egoism, pride, आहोपुरुषिका दर्पाद् या स्यात् संभावनात्मनि '. अहो-Alas! " अहो धिगर्थे शोके च, [करुणार्थे विषादयोः । संबोधने प्रशंसायां विस्मये पादपूरणे ॥] कारं कारं-" अभीक्ष्णं कृत्वा " doing again and again. It is a Namul form or gerund in अम् (vide apte's guide sec. 162.) पुराणि भिनत्ति इति पुरभिद्-God Shiva. The असुरs led by मयासुर prepared three big walls and remained in them safe from their enemies, the Gods. But महादेव, accompanied by other Gods, overcame them and destroyed these three पुरs and thus brought the demons to ruin. This episode has been described in many places, the above is common to all the places. (भागवत. 7–10)

संमुखयतः—संमुखं कुर्वतः-presenting before, aiming-gen. sing. from denominative participle from संमुख. स्मरस्य-of the god of love. स्वर्बालानां (देवाङ्गनानां) नयनानि एव सुमानि तेषां मालाः तासां अर्चनपदं (पूजास्थानम्)-The abode of worship or reverence by the garlands of flowers in the form of eyes of celestial damsels. भाले अनलः तस्य भसितजालं तस्य आस्पदम्-The receptacle of the mass of ashes of the fire on शिव's forehead. The reference is to the fire of the third eye on the forehead. of God Shiva.

Idea:—The evil done to great persons returns on its author, (Here the God of love tried to make the great God Shiva the butt of his arrows, but was himself reduced to ashes by the fire, on his forehead.)

85. मृदुलानि आसनानि-soft seats. चीत्कृतिः-refers to the particular cry of monkeys. आतिथेयी-(अतिथिसत्क्रिया)-hospitality. विपाटितानि refers to the scratches made by the monkeys in sport and in the act of greeting.

being (1) possessed of fibres (ii) Possessed of merits. स्वकीयानां गुणानां जालैः (ष. त.)-(1) by the net-work of its own threads. (ii) by the network (stock) of his own qualities. विवराणि मुद्रयन् (1) filling up the holes (गवाक्षादि) in the houses (ii) filling up the gaps (defects) of others. स्वकीयगुणजालैः is to be construed both with गुणवत्तामातन्वानः and विवराणि मुद्रयन्. The good man is here compared to a spider. It is well known that this insect prepares a cob-web, out of threads drawn out from its own body. A good man transforms a dunce also into one possessed of good qualities and hides his shortcomings. "द्राङ्-मङ्क्षु सपदि दृतम्" The word ऊर्णायु (spider) has been formed by adding the term युस् to ऊर्णा in the sense of possession, by ऊर्णाया युस् (Pan. 5-3-123.)

91. सज्जनः एव कार्पासः तस्य रक्षणे एकः (•अद्वितीयः) हुताशनः। The fire matchless in the protection of cotton in the form of a good man. एक is used in the sense of अद्वितीय. Vide न केवलं तद्गुरुरेकपार्थिवः क्षितावभूदेकधनुर्धरोऽपि सः ॥ परेषां दुःखं एव अग्निः तस्य शमने मारुतः-the wind in cooling the fire in the form of the pain of others. In this verse by लक्षणा the words रक्षणं and शमन mean exactly the opposite of the ordinary sense viz. भक्षण and प्रवर्धन respectively. This sense is to be followed because the expressed meaning is irrelevant here. लक्षणा consists in the superimposing of another meaning, when the primary meaning is not applicable; for details see-मम्मट's काव्य-प्रकाश 2. मुख्यार्थबाधे तद्योगे रूढितोऽथ प्रयोजनात्। अन्योर्थो लक्ष्यते यत्सा लक्षणारोपिताक्रिया.॥ There is an other reading also in the सुभाषित रत्नभांडागार which reads धक्षण or भक्षण for रक्षण and धमन for शमन thus leaving no necessity of resisting to any लक्षणा at all. The fire burning the cotton is proverbial cf.

न खलु न खलु बाण: संनिपात्योऽयमस्मिन्मृदुनि मृगशरीरे तूलराशाविवाग्नि: ।
Sak–I–10, so is the constant companionship of fire and wind and hence the aggravation of fire. cf.

मधुश्च ते मन्मथ साहचर्यादसावनुक्तोऽपि सहाय एव ।
समीरणो नदयिता भवेति व्यादिश्यते केन हुताशनस्य ॥

K. S. III 21

92. The epithets in the first line have a double meaning and the comparisons are made effective on account of puns. परेषां यद्गुह्यं तस्य गुप्ति: तस्मिन् निपुणं well-versed in protecting the गुह्य (1) secrets in the case of सज्जन & (2) private parts in the case (of ललिताम्बर) of others " रहस्योपस्थयोर्गुह्यम् ". गुणमयं (1) full of merits (2) full of threads. नितरामखिलै: समीहितं—P.P.P. from सम्+ईह्. desired–this is applicable to both–greatly desired by all. ललितं च तदम्बरं च a fine garment दूषयन्ति (1) spoil, blame (2) tear, gnaw. Instead of खला: some read खरा: But (" रलयो: अभेदात् " खल and खर (an ass) need not be distinguished from each other.

93. यश एव सौरभ्यं तस्य लशुन:–a garlic to the fragrance in the form of fame. Here the wicked man is compared to a garlic poetically. A garlic is sure to destroy any fragrance, so also a wicked man is sure to sully fame. शान्तिरेव शैत्यं तस्य हुताशन:–fire to the cold in the form of tranquillity or calmness of mind. "शमथस्तु शम: शान्ति:" हुतं अश्नाति इति हुताशन:–fire. Just as a fire is the enemy of cold so also a wicked man becomes the enemy of calmness of mind i. e. he will be ever perturbed, कारुण्यं एव कुसुमं तस्य आकाश:–the sky to the flowers in the form of compassion i. e. Just as आकाश will never produce flowers so also a wicked man will never put–

forth compassion. The idea suggested by " कुसुमाकाश " refers to the well-known अत्यन्ताभावs (absolute impossibility) in the following verse, मृगतृष्णाम्भसि स्नातः खपुष्पकृतशेखरः। एष वन्ध्यासुतो याति शशशृंगधनुर्धरः॥ He is ever merciless. सज्जनानां दुःखं-ददाति (v. l. दुःखलः-दुःखं लाति संपादयति) giving pain to the good.

94. कुसुमानि च पत्राणि च फलानि च तेषां आवलीनां भरं-The burden of clusters of flowers, leaves and fruits. घर्मस्यव्यथां pangs of heat. " घर्मोनिदाघः " शीताद् भवां रुजं pangs arising from cold. " स्त्री रुग्रुजा चोपतापरोगव्याधिगदामयाः " वदान्येषु गुरुः तस्मै-the foremost among the donors. " मां याचस्वेति वदति वदान्यः " " स्युर्वदान्यस्थूललक्ष्यदानशौण्डा बहुप्रदे. " नमस् requires the dat. of the person to whom salutation is offered. cf. हरचूडानिहितात्मने नमस्ते। v. k. 3)

Idea:—The tree is bowed down because he is the foremost among all those sacrificing their self for others.

c. f. स्वसुखनिरभिलाषः खिद्यसे लोकहेतोः
प्रतिदिनमथवा ते वृत्तिरेवं विधैव।
अनुभवति हि मूर्ध्ना पादपस्तीव्रमुष्णं
शमयति परितापं छायया संश्रितानाम्॥ S. 5-7.

Appli:—The best of self-sacrificers deserve salutations.

95. हालाहलं-deadly poison-one of the fourteen jewels churned out of the ocean described in the well-known verse, लक्ष्मीः कौस्तुभ etc. and later on drunk by the God Shiva. पिपासति-3rd sing. of the desiderative verb formed from पा to drink-desires to drink. कालानलः-(कालरूपः अनलः) This is the fire at the final deluge supposed to possess the greatest power of burning. cf. दग्धुं विश्वं दहनकिरणैर्नोदिता द्वादशार्काः। Ve. 3-8. परिचुचुम्बिषति

desiderative 3rd per. sing. from परि+चुम्ब्–to touch-to kiss. व्यालानां अधिपः–the lord of serpents. परिरब्धुं–inf. from परि+रभ् to embrace ,v. l. परिबन्द्धुं–to bind. अद्धा. (adv.) actually, really, manifestly. वशयितुं–inf. of the causal from वश्–to persuade–to win over. मनीषा–a desire.

Idea:—It is absolutely impossible to win over a wicked man.

96. " दीनो दरिद्रो दुर्गतोऽपि सः " दुःसहः मदः यस्य सः (बहु०) दुर्मदः तस्य–one who is unbearably haughty or proud. शुष्काणि सस्यानि–crops dried up owing to drought. औदार्यं प्रकटयतः–displaying generosity. It refers to the profuse pouring of the rain by the cloud on the mountains. मह्याः धराः ष. त. तावकः विवेकः–त्वदीयः विवेकः Here by ironical sense विवेक means अविवेकः. For the use of such लक्षणा See Bh. V. 1–91.

Idea:—Here the profuse charity of the cloud to the mountains, setting aside dry fields, is ironically condemned.

Appl:—Charity shown to the rich setting aside the poor, deserves condemnation. cf. दवदहनजटाल. Bh. V. 1–(36).

97. गुरवः–Great. जगदण्डम् (जगद्रूपं अण्डम्)–the whole universe. This universe is supposed to be the egg first created by the creator and then it produced this earth. प्रलयेऽप्यचलाः–firm–undaunted–even at the time of the world deluge. cf. अपि स्फुटति विन्ध्याद्रौ वाति वा प्रलयानले। गुरुशास्त्रानुगो मार्गः परित्याज्यो न धीमता ॥ (योगवासिष्ठ).

Idea:—The magnanimous are the greatest of all.

98. बीजाकृ–to sow seeds. पवने चित्रं निर्माति etc.–Sowing seeds in the sky is equivalent to no-sowing; drawing pictures in the wind and lines in water are as good

as not doing so; similarly paying respect to the wicked is as good as not paying it.

Idea:—Respect paid to the wicked, is fruitless.

v. l. व्योमनि वापं कुरुते (or शंबां कुरुते), चित्रं निर्माति यत्नत: सलिले । स्नपयति पवनं सलिलैर्य: क्षुद्रे चरति सत्कारम् ॥

शंबां कुरुते–He ploughs the fields (in the sky.) शम्बां–" क्षेत्रभक्ति-कृषिविभागम् "

स्नपयति–Caus. 3rd. Sing. from स्ना to bathe cf. हालाहलं खलु Bh. V. I–98.

99. लेढि is present 3rd. per. sing. of लिह् to lick and जिघ्रति of घ्रा to smell. आसनं उन्नतं करोति–means, raises his seat (of course by placing the necklace below its haunches). This aims at showing that pearls cast before swine are not valued.. In the present case the necklace of jewels is immensely valuable but what of that to an ape ? When he finds that it cannot be eaten, he throws it away; because it is worthless from his viewpoint. cf. किं मिष्टमन्नं खरसूकराणाम् ।

Idea:—A monkey does not realise the value of a necklace of jewels.

Some editions read आननम् for आसनम् in line 4. This is also a good reading. This enables one to form a mental picture of the monkey. When it first licks the necklace, then smells and throws it away (finding it of no use) and then raises its head as if to express that it is worthless in his opinion in the act of mocking.

अनल्पं जल्पते इति–who is very talkative. विकसितं वदनं यस्या: with a blooming face. The above is the expressed meaning wherein the action of a bee leaving a lotus–

plant that loves it in inspite of its shortcomings is condemned for its faithlessness. This verse is also to be understood in another sense viz. as an advice to a fickle lover who loves his lady who is attached to him inspite of his numerous shortcomings. This अलंकार is known as समासोक्ति in Sanskrit rhetoric and is defined by मम्मट as परोक्तिर्भेदकैः श्लिष्टैः समासोक्तिः (The description of another thing [परोक्ति] by paranomastic (श्लिष्टैः) adjectives (भेदकैः) is called समासोक्ति). Hence besides the one interpretation that has been given, there is also another explanation possible. Here a भ्रमर will mean a truthless, dishonest lover, whereas the सरोजिनी will mean the lady who is in love with him and tries to please him in all possible ways. In that case मलिनेऽपि रागपूर्णा etc. will mean that she is attached to you although you are truthless, deceitful. She looks smilingly at you although you are very talkative. (Talkative persons are supposed to be insincere in love-matters), she loves you, though you are fickle-minded. How would you then, O lover, abandon your lady ?

adjectives	as applied to the bee.	applied to the lover.	adjectives	as applied to सरोजिनं	as applied to the lady.
मलिन	black	faithless	रागपूर्णां	Red-coloured	full of love
अनल्पजल्पे	Constantly humming	very talkative (in dication of fickle-mindedness)	विकसितवदनां	with blooming lotuses	with smiling face.

चपले	active (physically)	unstable in mind	सरसां	full of honey	full of amorousness or affection.

101. मलिनतां भज्–to be blackened, to be disgraced. इदं किं विचित्रम् what wonder is there ? परस्मै इदं परार्थं (च. त.) स्वस्मै इदं स्वार्थम्. कालिमानं. Here the illustration is based on the pun on the word कालिमन्.

Idea:—Begging money of rich people for selfish purposes brings infamy.

102. जनक: सानुविशेषः The father of sandal is a particular सानु (summit) of the mountain मलय i. e. it has a low descent. जाति: काष्ठम्–Its caste is wood which is not so honourable. It keeps company with the serpents and hence this is also a serious defect. Thus all the three ways by which a man attains greatness viz. descent, position and companionship being absent in the case of sandal, naturally its greatness is retarded, but it reaches greatness only through its intrinsic greatness not with–standing the presence of the above–mentioned three serious defects.

Idea:—Sandal is great only because of its intrinsic merits.

103. " हन्त हर्षेऽनुकम्पायाम् " here it shows अनुकम्पा. गुणानां ग्रामः (multitude) तस्य अर्जनम् obtaining a multitude of virtues. चेत्–if. स्वात्मनः उपस्करणं ornament to oneself. भावाः–qualities, things. शोभाभरैः संभृताः (lit. nourished) full of great beauty. सज्जसि–from the root सस्ज् to get ready. तैरेव कलेः वर्तनम् (वृत्तिः)–quarrels maintain themselves on these beautiful qualities. The idea is that quarrels grow in this world on account of the possession of

merits. कलेवरं पुष्णाति-तस्य adj. to कलिः whose body is day by day growing robust and hence the quarrels in the world increase daily. The कलि is said to be waxing stronger because it is being powerful day by day as it advances. This is based on the belief that the कलि age began on the day when Shri Krishna breathed his last and since that day it has been growing more and more powerful. Here कलि is personified and hence is described as कलेवरपुष् [The कलि is said to have begun on the day on which श्रीकृष्ण went to वैकुण्ठ when the great Bear entered the constellation मघा. It consists of 4,32000 years of men and it began on the 13th of Feb. 3102 B. C.]

Idea:—Do not cultivate any merits for it is the root of all dissensions.

The reading वर्धनं for वर्तनम् is not so happy because कलेवरपुष: already has the idea of वर्धन, वर्तनम् is much better because, although the body of कलि is fat, if its source of livelihood वर्तनम् (वृत्तिः) is stopped it will wane immediately. Our deliberate negligence in acquiring merits is the only way of emaciating Kali.

104. धूमायिताः—P. P. P. of the denominative from धूम—Turned smoky. दलितानि (bloomed) अरविन्दानि यासु ताः (adj. to दिशः) in which the lotuses are blown open. v. l. ललितारविन्दाः—in which there are charming lotuses; of course this reading is inapplicable as without the spring there can be no charm in lotuses. गन्धस्य वाहाः—गन्धवाहाः—winds. अन्तरेण " without " requires the acc. e. g. तत्वं किमपि काव्यानां जानाति विरलो भुवि । मार्मिकः को मरन्दानामन्तरेण मधुव्रतम् । Bh. V. 1-117. मृदूनि ताम्राणि दलानि येषां, ते आम्राः तेषु मञ्जु गुञ्जन्तः मधुव्रताः (bees) यस्मिन् सः-एतादृश हे मधो - (मधु व्रतं

(भक्ष्ये) येषां ते मधुव्रताः)-spring in which the bees are humming melodiously on the mango trees whose leaves are tender and red. v. l. मृदुताम्रदलाम्र मञ्जु गुञ्जन् मधुव्रत मधो. मृदुताम्रदलाम्र and मञ्जु...मधुव्रत qualify मधो-the meaning will be similarly taken. v. l. मृदुलाम्रदलाम्र. Here आम्र after मृदुल is superfluous. v. l. मृदुजालकलाम्र-(मृदुजालकल-आम्र) मञ्जुगुञ्जन्मधुव्रत मधो—This reading yields a farfetched meaning मृदु जालकं (कलिकाजालं) तद् लाति (आदत्ते) एतादृश आम्र-i. e. a tree, putting on the cluster of tender blossoms. मञ्जु ..व्रतम् qualifies त्वां कोकिलस्य is to be construed with देह in the 2nd line. Here there is दूरान्वय-दोष.

Idea:—Spring is a great pleasure-giver, without him lotuses & cuckoos will be scorched on account of summer heat.

Appl:—The value of a really deserving man is known only in his absence.

105. भिन्ना—P. P. P. from भिद् to break. करेजायन्ते इति करजाः (nails) तेषां अग्राणि तेषां जाग्रतः (active) उद्दामाः शौर्यस्य निकराः तैः—with a great deal of valour, active and prominent at the ends of their nails. "करटः करिगण्डे स्यात्" हेमः । करटिभ्रमेण-Mistaking rocks for elephants. दैवे पराचि-when fate is adverse. पराच् adj. unfavourable. कुत्रापि नापि खलु हा पिशितस्य लेशः । Here नापि=न+आपि passive 3rd per. sing. aorist from आप i. e. did not obtain. "पिशितं तरसं मांसं" v. l. लिलिहे-Pass. Perf. of लिह् was licked.

Idea:—Under adverse circumstances even though a lion puts forth the best of his valour yet he does not get even a bit of an elephant's flesh.

Appli:—प्रतिकूलतामुपगते हि विधौ विफलत्वमेति बहुसाधनता ।

106. गर्जितम् refers to the thundering of clouds. मनाग meansईषद्-a little. "किंचिदीषन्मनागल्पे.' निशायाः अर्धं जातस्य

अस्य–though half a night old. (Pan. कालाः परिमाणिना 2–2–5) द्राक्–at once, quickly. v. l. अतिभृशम् greatly. निभृतम्–secretly. आकुंच्य-gerund of आ+कुञ्च् 6. P.-Having contracted.

Idea and Appli:—cf. Bh. V. I–61.

107. दिव्या मतिः यस्य सः (बहु.) of divine (celestial) intellect (said ironically.) गुणेषु पक्षपातः (स. त.) Partiality for qualities (said ironically). अहनि च निशायां च अहर्निशम्–always, constantly. शालिन्- adj. generally used at the end of a compound meaning possessed of. Hence गुणशालिनः means men possessed of good qualities. The intended meaning is that the wicked always trouble the meritorious persons. This is technically known as व्याजस्तुति i. e praise resulting in censure.

108. अग्रे in front of वि+विच् (3–7 U) to separate, divide. Gerund of this root is विविच्य. पापः आत्मा यस्य सः– whose self is sinful. हत–wretched. अलम् used with instrumental in the sense of निवारण. "अलं भूषणपर्याप्तिशक्तिवारणभूमसु" [This is an example of an आक्षेपालंकार, which consists in denying what is intended with the object of intimating something in particular. (see का० प्र० X)] " अथवा " is used to correct or modify the former statement. (vide Apte's Guide Sec. 245 a) दीर्घे किं न सहस्रधाहमथवा रामेण किं दुष्करम् (U. 6–40) Here the author leaves aside his first thought of relating the biography of a wicked man intimating that it is horrible and hence he is desisting from doing so.

109. खलानां समागमः–companionship with the wicked. आनंदः एव मृगः (कर्म.) तस्य दावाग्निः, दावश्चासौ अग्निश्च " दवदावौ वनारण्यवह्नी " forest conflagration to the deer in the form of joy. शीलं एव शाखी (कर्म०)-a tree in the form of character

मदयुक्त: द्विप:-(शाखपार्थिवादि स.) like a rutting elephant to the tree in the form of one's character. ज्ञानं एव दीप: (कर्म०) तस्य महावायु:-like a hurricane to the lamp in the form of knowledge.

Idea. The companionship with the wicked, mars our joy, destroys our character and extinguishes our knowledge. आनन्द is metaphorically supposed to be a मृग, so also शील to be a शाखिन् and ज्ञान to be a दीप.

110. साधूनां हितं तस्य प्रत्यूहकर्म–तस्मिन् कुशला: "विघ्नोऽन्तराय: प्रत्यूह:"–clever in the act of putting impediments in the welfare of the good. निर्गतं आग: यस्मात् स:–निरागा: तेषाम् (बहु.) " आगोऽपराधो मन्तुश्च । " प्राणान् is used in the plural, (Apte's Guide Sec. 6,) because they are five in number–प्राण, अपान, व्यान, उदान and समान and are said to occupy the following places in the body. हृदि प्राणो गुदेऽपान: समानो नाभिमण्डले उदान: कण्ठदेशस्थो व्यान: सर्वशरीरग: ।।

111. " रसज्ञा रसना जिह्वा " रसनाया: मिषेण in the guise of the tongue. विनिवेशित is the p. p. p. of वि+नि+विश् cau. अवलीढ is p. p. p. of अवलिह्–licked, bit. नास्ति मन्त्र: येषां ते (बहु.) (1) who are not cured by magical charms. (2) Unless good counsel is given to them.

112. (This whole verse is ironical). उन्नतम्–noble, here by व्यंग्यार्थ means "base." अमलम्–clear, unstained, by व्यंग्यार्थ notorious. आशिष:–blessings, here curses. यावज्जीवम् so long as life lasts, is a Namul form formed by the Sutra यावति विन्दजीवो: (Pan. 3–4–30) (यावाज्जीव: तावन्तं कालम्) सखे also then means शत्रो.

113. अविरतं परकार्यकृतां सतां वच: मधुरिमातिशयेन अमृतं (इव) अपि च मानसं अंबुनिधि: (इव) यश: विमलशारदचंदिरचंद्रिका । परेषां कार्याणि कुर्वन्ति ते परकार्यकृत:-तेषां obligers of others. मधुरिम्ण: अतिशय: तेन excess of sweetness. शरदि भव: शारद: by the Sutra

संधिवेलाद्यृतुनक्षत्रेभ्योऽण् (Pan. 4-3-16) विमलश्च असौ शारद: चंदिरः (चन्द्रः) तस्य चंद्रिका–the moonlight of the clear autumnal moon. मानसं (mind) is like the sea–in its expanse, greatness. This points to the magnanimity of the man. The autumnal sky is typically clear.

114. कुसुमानां आकर:—mine of flowers i. e. spring. सञ्जीवयिता–1st future 3rd per. sing. from the causal of जीव् with सम्–will restore to life. समधायि—Pass. Aorist 3rd per. sing. from धा with सम्–was aimed at–i.e. discharged. शौभिकेन—by a fowler.

This is an example .of how man proposes and God disposes.

115. निर्गता: गुणा: यस्मात् स: निर्गुण:–devoid of merits. विपुल: आडम्बरः यस्य स: विपुलाडम्बर:-of ample ostentatious display i e. set off by fine (outward) display. आपाते रम्या पुष्पाणां श्री: तया शोभित:–adorned by the beauty of flowers charming for the present moment.

116. सद:–An assembly–a meeting. " आस्थानं...सद: " कटुवर्णै:–Harsh alphabets. (कटवश्च ते वर्णाश्च तै:) विषयै:–sensual objects. पङ्कै:–the plural does not denote any thing in particular. Perhaps it is used for euphony with जनै:, वर्णै: and विषयै: Here in this verse the verb भाति is to be construed with every idea.

117. Exp. किमपि–indescribable. मार्मिक:-an appreciator. मरन्द:–honey. For अन्तरेण and मधुव्रत see Bh. V. 1–104.

118. निर्गता त्रपा (shame;) यस्मात् स: निस्त्रप:–Shameless. In this verse the word निस्त्रप is the most important one as it is the root cause of the double meanings of the following words. सरजस्कां–रजसा सह–(1) full of pollen (applicable to the केतकी creeper) (2) a woman in

menstruation (applicable in the case of a shameless man who is intended to be condemned.) पाण्डुवर्णां-पाण्डुः वर्णः यस्याः सा (1) of dusty yellowish complexion, (2) of pale colour (It shows palour and consequent weakness of a woman who is therefore not proper for enjoyment.) कण्टकानां प्रकरैः अन्विताम्-(1) accompanied by a number of thorns. (The केतकी possessed of the thorns.) (2) possessed of rough hair. (in the case of a woman.) रोलम्ब–O bee.

Idea:—It refers to a shameless man who enjoys a woman in menstruation and to a bee who enjoys a केतकी of the type described above.

119. Four worthless things are pointed out in this verse. तानः-variation in notes in a song. रागः refers to any variety of a song. दानं–means "rut", "intoxication," "Ichor."

120. स्वतः of their own accord. परतः through the medium of others. "आमोदः सोऽतिनिर्हारी." हि–indeed. The idea in the last line is–we are not required to take an oath to prove the existence of musk. विभाव्यते–Is made known; present causal passive 3rd per. sing. of भू with वि.

The good qualities of men, come to light of their own accord and not through (the medium of) others. The fragrance of musk is not indeed made known by oath.

121. गर्वं मा (अ) यासीः–Do not be proud. मौलिः-the best (lit. the head) because 'head' is the best limb of the body. गिरेः गहने गुहायां in the den in the forest on the mountain. स्वजनकः–the father of musk i.e. the कस्तूरीमृग which possesses the musk and hence is hunted by the

fowlers, his existence being made known everywhere by the diffusion of its fragrance.

Idea. O कस्तूरि do not be proud, of your fragrance which brings death to your father.

Appl. People should not feel proud of that wealth which they have obtained at the sacrifice of their near and dear ones.

122. दूरीकृ-विमलीकृ-चुलुकीकृ बहुलीकृ are all च्वि formations in the sense of अभूततद्भाव i.e. changing a thing into that, which was not before. कुत्सिता मतिः (कर्म.) विगतः मलः यस्मात् तत् (बहु.) adj. चेतः. to चिरंतन adj. of long standing. चुलुकीकरोति-(चुलुक-a mouthful) swallows i.e. destroys. cf सत्संगतिः कथय किं न करोति पुंसाम्. सतां संगः is to be construed with every clause.

123. अनवरतः यः परोपकारः तेन व्यग्रीभवति अमलं चेतः येषाम्-तेषाम् (बहु.) adj. to महताम्-of the great whose pure mind is always engrossed in the incessant (performance of) charitable actions. आपाते काटवं येषां तानि adj. to वचनानि-whose bitterness (unpleasantness) is felt only in the beginning (afterwards it is wholesome as the medicine). The adjectives can be beautifully interpreted to refer to वचन as well as भेषज.

124. व्यागुंजन्तः ये मधुकराः तेषां पुंजैः मंजु (adv.) गीता. (adj.) to स्तुति-the praise that is sung by the clusters of sweetly humming bees. उदयन् यो नयः (विनयः) तस्य अतिरेकः-Excess of modesty resulting from it (the praise). अवनौ रोहन्ति ते-trees. आभूमीतलं नताः कंधराः येषां तानि-bending their necks to (reach) the ground.

Idea:—the trees (which are personified) bend down their neck and touch the ground by their branches through modesty on hearing their praise sung by the bees. This is a fine example of उत्प्रेक्षा.

In मृतस्य लिप्सा–मृतस्य is कर्मणि षष्ठी i. e. मृत is to be the कर्म of लिप्सा–लब्धुं इच्छा–लिप्सा a desiderative noun.–the desire of getting back a dead man. कृपणस्य दित्सा–Here कृपणस्य is कर्तरिषष्ठी ie. कृपण is to be an agent of the action of giving–दातुं इच्छा–the desire to give, in the mind of a miserly man. (शास्त्र) विरुद्धो मार्गः विमार्गः तेन गच्छति सा विमार्गगा–a wanton woman. विधातुः सृष्टिः ष. त. तस्यां पूर्वं दृष्टा दृष्टपूर्वा सुप्सुप्समास.

126. राज्ञः प्रियाः–राजप्रियाः favourites of the king i.e. the moon i.e. loved by the moon. कैरविण्यः–night lotuses. " सिते कुमुदकैरवे " कैरवाणि सन्ति येषां—the night-lotus-plants. मधुपैः-with the bees-drunkards. The poet hints at the second meaning by the word मधुप. Perhaps he thereby desires to have a glimpse at the contemporary court life. cf. यथा स्त्रीणां तथा वाचां साधुत्वे (शुद्धत्वे) दुर्जनो जनः । U. 1–5

127. उद्गता शृंखला यस्य सः—unruly—unchained.

128. This verse is a fine example of the heroic sentiment. दोर्दण्ड... ..मण्डलं adj. to त्वां. दोषौ दण्डौ इव–दोर्दण्डौ–तयोः द्वयं तेन कुण्डलीकृतं यद् लसत्कोदण्डं तस्य चण्डाशुगैः (terrible arrows) ध्वस्तं उद्दण्डविपक्षमण्डलं येन सः बहु.–तं [कुण्डलीकृतं–turned into a circle by drawing the string i e. bent round. लसत्कोदण्डं–brilliant bow. " धनुश्चापौ धन्वशरासनकोदण्डकार्मुकम् " आशु गच्छन्ति–आशुगाः–quick goers i.e. arrows. उद्दण्ड–उद्गतौ दण्डौ येषां ते–Powerful or mighty. विरुद्धः पक्षः–विपक्षः enemy.]– Who has destroyed the circle of his mighty foes by the terrible arrows discharged from his shining bow bent round by his arms. रणस्य मध्ये–मध्येरणम् अव्य.–In the battle. [वल्गद्गाण्डिवाद् मुक्तं यत् काण्डवलयं तस्य ज्वालानां आवलीनां ताण्डवेन भ्रश्यत् यत् खाण्डवं तस्मिन् रुष्टः (angry) पाण्डवः (i.e. अर्जुनः)–तं [वल्गद् गाण्डिव–noisy bow of अर्जुन named गाण्डिव–Mythological

allusion :- Agni once approached shri Krishna and Arjuna and begged of them the खाण्डव forest by eating which he hoped to be cured of the disease caused by eating too much of sacrificial food. The boon was granted by them and Agni was cured of his disease. Being thus pleased with shri Krishna and Arjuna, he gave them as presents the वज्रनाभ चक्र and the गाण्डिव bow respectively.

Mbh. Adi. 224–225 adhyayas.

काण्डानां वलयं circle of arrows. "काण्डोऽस्त्रीदण्डबाणार्व" ज्वालावली-ताण्डव-dance of the series of flames. भ्रश्यत्-being destroyed-perishing] अर्जुन who was indignant in the खाण्डव forest which was destroyed by the movement (lit. dance) of the series of flames (arising) from the circle of arrows discharged from the twanging bow.

Idea:—Your sight reminds one of अर्जुन.

129. खण्डितानां नेत्राणि एव कञ्जानि तेषां आलयः तेषां मञ्जु रञ्जने पण्डिताः-Expert in (giving) sweet amusement, in giving charm to the rows of lotuses in the form of the eyes of insulted ladies. A खण्डिता is that woman whose husband's love is privately directed to another lady. She is very indignant at her husband for his infidelity. But her husband propitiates her and falls at her feet at sunrise. Hence the rays of the sun are said to cheer up the spirits of a खण्डिता lady. cf. मेघ. 39. खण्डिता is defined in साहित्यदर्पण as follows:-पार्श्वमेति प्रियो यस्या अन्यसंभोगचिह्नितः। सा खण्डितेति कथिता धीरैरीर्ष्या कषायिता ॥ S. D. 114. के (in water) जायन्ते-कञ्जानि (Ir-reg. समासः) मण्डिताः अखिलदिक्प्रान्ताः (दिग्भागाः) यैः ते- who adorned all the nooks and corners of the quarters.

Notes शान्तविलास.

1. विशाला या विषयाणां (objects of sense) अटवी (forest) तस्याः वलयं (circle) तस्मिन् लग्नः यः दावानलः (forest conflagration) तेन प्रसृत्वरा (Spreading) या शिखानां (flames) आवली तया विकलितम् (afflicted) adj. to मनः । प्रसृत्वरा–प्रसरणशीला. The word is formed by adding the affix क्वरप् to प्र+सृ in the sense of agent, possessing that habit, by Sutra इण्नशजिसर्तिभ्यः क्वरप् (Pan 3-2-163) अमंदं (incessantly) मिलन्ती इन्दिरा (beauty) यस्मिन् सः (बहु.) adj. to चंदिरः । निखिलायाः माधुर्याः (loveliness) मन्दिरं-तस्मिन् । मुकुन्दस्य मुखं एव चन्दिरः (कर्म.) तस्मिन् । 'चन्दिरोऽनेकपे चन्द्रे' इति विश्वः । चकोरायताम् is the potential 3rd pers. sing. of the denominative from चकोर showing "acting like", hence meaning 'may it act like a चकोर' i. e. long for the moon in the form of the face of श्रीकृष्ण. This is formed by the Sutra उपमानादाचारे (Pan 3-1-10) The चकोर is conventionally supposed to long for the appearance of the moon, so that it might drink her nectar. This idea has also been referred to in Bh. V. 1-4.

Idea:—May my mind long for a vision of मुकुन्द.

2. जलधेः नन्दिन्याः (Laxmi) नयने एव नीरजे (lotuses) तयोः आलम्बनं (support) तत्संबोधनम् । Laxmi is only delighted at the sight of विष्णु. ज्वलन् (burning) यः ज्वलनः (fire) तस्य जित्वरः (conqueror-i. e. more scorching than fire) यः ज्वरभरः (excess of pain) तस्य त्वरा (keenness) तेन भङ्गुरः (fragile) adj. to अहम् । जित्वर is formed like प्रसृत्वर. See notes on the above stanza. भङ्गुर also shows "the habit of breaking" and has been formed by the Sutra भञ्जभासमिदो घुरच् (Pan. 3-2-161) प्रभाते (विकसतः) जलजस्य उज्जमन् (appearing) यः गरिमा (expanse) तस्य गर्वस्य सर्वंकषैः (नाशकैः). adj.

to लोचनैः। The cyes remove the pride of the bigness of the lotus i.e. they are even bigger than the lotus. जगतः त्रितयं (a collection of three worlds) तस्य रोचनैः (pleasing) adj. to लोचनैः। शिशिरय = make me cool. The plural लोचनैः is justified when it is interpreted as 'glances' and not "the eyes".

[**Idea**:—Consol me because I am immersed in worries.] "कादम्बिनी मेघमाला" It literally means a row of clouds. Here however by लक्षणा (for लक्षणा vide notes on verse 91 of प्रा. वि.) it should mean Krishna himself who is always described as being possessed of the श्याम colour. The incident described in the poem is the one dealing with the गोपिकावस्त्रहरण when Shri-Krishna seated himself on a कदम्ब tree and played with the Gopis. cf. तासां वासांस्युपादाय नीपमारुह्य सत्वरः। हसद्भिः प्रहसन् बालैः परिहासमुवाच ह ॥ Bhag.-X. 22-9 तरुणातप meaning scorching heat, here of course of the worldly affairs. Krishna is supposed to remove the distresses of his devotees, even when remembered once. Cf. यस्य स्मरणमात्रेण जन्म-संसारबन्धनात्। विमुच्यते नमस्तस्मै विष्णवे प्रभविष्णवे ॥ Krishna, like other Gods, is always described and painted as being possessed of a halo of lustre round his head and this is referred to in the second line. विद्युतां शतैः hundreds of lightnings. अभङ्गुरा तनूनां त्विट् येषां तानि adj. to विद्युतां शतानि. The lustre of whose bodies is not transitory like that of the lightning. Mark here the आधिक्य of उपमेय i. e. तनुत्विष् over उपमान the विद्युत्, resulting into what is termed in rhetorics as the व्यतिरेक. There is also अतिशयोक्ति clearly visible herein. कलिन्द-नगस्य नन्दिनी-तस्याः तटे (वर्तमानः) यः सुरद्रुमः-तस्मिन् आलम्बते-सा-Resorting to the celestial tree on the bank of the daughter of the mountain कलिन्द "कालिन्दी सूर्यतनया यमुना शमनस्वसा". The कदम्ब tree on which Krishna seated himself is here called the celestial tree because of its unparalleled luck in being the resort of कृष्ण. This verse vividly pictures before our mind's eye the scene on the bank of the Jumna where on the नीप tree कृष्ण is sitting with an object of joking with garments left on the bank by the गोपीs who are taking naked bath in the Jumna. Jagannatha in various places associates the blue line of clouds with Shri Krishna. (Cf. Stanzas 5,8 etc. of this विलास) मदीयां मतिं चुम्बते सा lit. one that touches my intellect i.e. becomes an object of my contemplation. का अपि means indescribable. This word suggests that the present कादम्बिनी is infinitely superior to the ordinary कादम्बिनी (row of clouds.) inasmuch as the latter possesses only one lightning with transitory lustre but the former is encircled by hundreds of lightnings with everlasting lustre. Hence such a कादम्बिनी is nothing except श्रीकृष्ण himself. This is the opening stanza of the रसगंगाधर.

Idea:–May I contemplate over Lord Shri Krishna.

4. कलिन्दगिरिनन्दिन्या: (यमुनाया:) तटे यद् वनस्य अन्तरं (the interior of the forest) तत् । भासयन् filling with lustre. Shri Krishna is supposed to have sanctified the regions surrounding Muttra by his divine presence there. प्राणिनां पथि गतागतश्रमभरं हरन्–Removing the burden of the exhaustion due to the (frequent) going and coming in the journey. पथि here means "the worldly path." and गतागत to "the Cycle of births and deaths" and then the whole meaning aptly applies to श्रीकृष्ण who liberates his devotee from the "Cycle of births and deaths." लतावलीनां शतेन आवृत:–Encircled by hundreds of

rows of creepers. लता: refers to the gold-complexioned गोपीs who encircle श्रीकृष्ण at the time of the famous रासक्रीडा. See (Bh. 10-33) आशु-instantly. रुचा संभृतः-enhanced by splendour. तमालद्रुमः-a tree named तमाल with a dark bark; here inwardly it refers to श्रीकृष्ण whose complexion is like that of a तमाल tree. Who else can be instataneous remover of the fatigue but श्रीकृष्ण ?

5. नवीन: i. e. लोकोत्तर:. Here in this verse all the epithets are not applicable to the जलधर hence it is called the नवीन जलधर; but on the other hand it can be said that no जलधर has power to bring about any of the actions referred to in the verse. So, naturally, all the actions referred to their only agent i. e. श्रीकृष्ण. Hence जलधर refers to श्रीकृष्ण. His dark complexion which resembles that of a cloud also points to the same. Besides the word नवीन (जलधर) is also significant. ज्योत्स्नामय्य: या: नवसुधा: ताभि:-with new nectar full of moonlight-splendour. ज्योत्स्नामयी full of moonlight जटिलयन्-Pres. Parti. of the denom. from जटिल lit. making matted i. e. pervading, filling. जगज्जालम्-the net of the world i. e. the surface of the earth.

त्रय: विधाः यस्य सः तम्-of three kinds-त्रिविधसन्ताप refers to the three-fold troubles of the worldly people i. e. आधिभौतिक-Elemental trouble due to the transmigratory existence. आधिदैविक-Godly-pertaining to Gods. आध्यात्मिक spiritual-pertaining to the soul When a person is liberated from the clasp of three troubles he acquires final beatitude. प्रशमयन्-Pre. Past. from the caus. of शम् with प्र. removing-putting a stop to. नताः निखिलवृन्दारकाः (all Gods) तैः वृतः-surrounded by all the Gods that bowed down (to him)-" वृन्दारका दैवतानि " स्वान्तस्य

ध्वान्तम्–the darkness i. e. (ignorance) of my heart. तिरयतु–may destroy.

6. ग्रीष्मे यः चण्डकरः तस्य मण्डलं (disc), तस्य भीष्मज्वालाः इव संसरणं (worldly existence) तेन तापिता मूर्तिः यस्य सः एवं विधस्य मे। चण्डाः कराः यस्य सः the Sun. भीष्मज्वालाः–the terrible heat-flame. संसरण noun from सृ with सम्–transmigratory existence. It is so called because a person is required to move from one birth to another according to his merits and demerits (thus through 8400000 existences) until he gets मोक्ष. प्रावृषेण्यः प्रावृषि भवः

वृष्णिषु वरेण्यः (श्रेष्ठः)–the best of वृष्णिs i.e. यादवs–श्रीकृष्ण. वृष्णि is the name of the ancestor of श्रीकृष्ण.

The idea is that just as the cloud in the rainy season allays the heat of the tormenting summer-sun so also may श्रीकृष्ण liberate me from this transmigratory existence.

7. न विद्यते पारः यस्य सः shoreless–unlimited-difficult to be crossed. विषमं विषयरूपं अरण्यं तस्य या सरणिः तस्याम्–In the path leading to the uneven forest in the form of the worldly pleasures. भ्रामं भ्रामं–णमुल् having frequently wandered. repetition shows frequency. विगलित विरामः यस्मिन् कर्मणि तत्तया–in a manner in which rest is lost i.e. restlessly. जडा मतिः यस्य सः तस्य मम–dull minded. तरणेः ' द्युमणिस्तरणिर्मित्रः " तनया (यमुना) तस्याः तीरे निलयः (home) यस्य सः–adj. to हरिनवतमालः । हरिः एव नवतमालः ।

8. जलधेः कन्यका–The daughter of the Ocean i. e. Goddess लक्ष्मी. लक्ष्मी is one of the fourteen jewels churned out by Gods and demons from the Ocean. Cf लक्ष्मीकौस्तुभपारिजातकसुराधन्वतरिश्चन्द्रमाः etc. लीलया सह यथा स्यात् तथा इति सलीलम्–Sportively. लग्नः P. P. from लग् (attached to or embraced) प्रियंगुलता is a tender-creeper. It is the

convention of the Sanskrit poets that सहकार (a mango tree) and अतिमुक्तलता, तमाल and प्रियंगुलता are the types of loving couples and hence the significance of the simile in the present verse. देहस्य अवसानसमये–at the time of the end of the body. अवसान–Termination–noun from सो with अव to finish (4. P.) अरविन्दं नाभौ यस्य सः-one who has a lotus in his naval. Mythology says that a lotus rose from the naval of विष्णु and from it, came out the four-faced God, Creator–ब्रह्मदेव.

9. नयनयोः आनन्दस्य सन्दोहः (mass) तस्य तुन्दिलीकरणे क्षमा (able)–able to increase (तुन्दिलीकरणे) the mass of joy to the eyes. (तुन्दिल lit. means corpulent). तिरयतु may it remove. आशु means immediately.

10. सुधा इव मधुरा Sweet like ambrosia. निर्गतः मलः यस्याः सा, तया वाचा–pure. This वाक् is nothing but the वेदs which are supposed to be the breath of God. शिक्षा Consists of the realization of the non-difference between God (सः) and ego. (अहम्) Viz. तत्त्वमसि Ch. VI–12. अहंभाव: the notion of considering oneself as different from the Supreme Being. अदाः Aorist 2nd pers. sing. of दा to give.

अहंभावावृतः–overwhelmed by ego. निर्गता त्रपा यस्मात् सः shameless. आगसां शतम् hundred faults. स्वीयेषु men favoured by God. त्वत्+तः (ablative) मत्तः (ablative). मत्तः arrogant.

11. सुरपुरी the city of Gods i.e. अमरावती which is supposed to be the place of unmixed joy. मेरु is supposed to be the highest mountain of gold (see Bhagawata 5–16–7) पारावाराणां परम्परा line of oceans. 'पारावारः सरित्पतिः' the oceans are supposed to be seven in number encircling the seven द्वीपs surrounding the मेरु mountain.

According to "Bhagawat Purana" (5–20) मेरु is in the centre. Surrounding this mountain there is the country known as जम्बुद्वीप (on which we are living) surrounded by क्षीरोद. Surrounding this क्षीरोदधि there is the प्लक्षद्वीप surrounded by इक्षुरसोद. This will be made clear by the following diagram:—

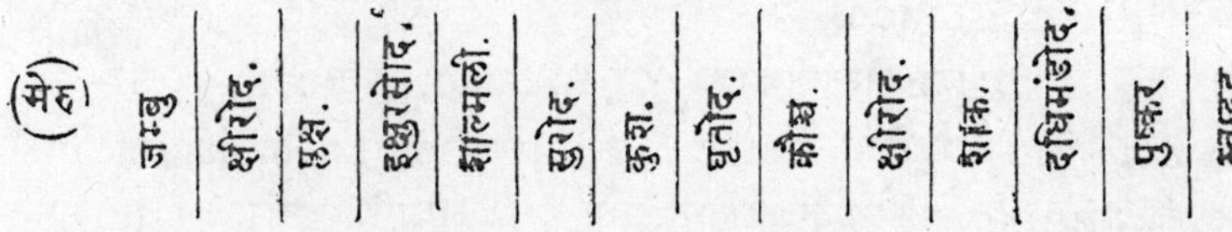

आधि is mental trouble where-as व्याधि is physical pain. पराहत: overwhelmed. रसायनं medicine. रस: taste. शून्यैः fruitless: v. 1. आधिव्याधिजरापराहत. overpowered by mental and physical pain and old-age.

12. गणिका–a prostitute. The story of the गणिका पिङ्गला has been narrated in Bhagawat 11-8 Verses 22–43. She attained to the knowledge of her "Self" According to her profession she was waiting for a customer but till late at night she got none and through despondency she realized the truth, the real पुरुष was her own "Self" and none else.

cf :—सन्तं समीपे रमणं रतिप्रदं, वित्तप्रदं नित्यमिमं विहाय ।
अकामदं दुःखभयाधिशोकमोहप्रदं तुच्छमहं भजेऽज्ञा ॥ Bhag.
11-8-31

अजामिल was a sinner. He was a man of impure conduct but was ultimately saved, when he saw three persons with nooses in hands coming to kill him, knowing that Death would soon overtake him he called aloud his dearest son Narayana (Bhagwat 6-Adhy. 1-2) Immediately the servant of Vishnu arrived and drove away those (servants) of यम. He was then filled with remorse for his evil way of leading life and obtained मुक्ति. vide हैमं विमानमारुह्य ययौ यत्र प्रियः पतिः ।

भवः एव मरुगर्तं : the desert in the form of the worldly existence. सीदन्—drooping—desponding सर्वथा न उपेक्ष्य : It does not become you to neglect me altogether i.e., lend some help to me to raise myself from this worldly existence.

13. "मृद्वीका गोस्तनी द्राक्षा" रस् to taste. सिता sugar. सम्+अश् to eat and समशिता eaten (to my heart's satisfaction) स्फीतं—ample. स्वर्यातेन कतिधा सुधा अपि अधायि स्वर्गते : i.e. स्वः यातः—gone to heavens. कतिधा many a time. अधायि passive aorist of धे to suck. रम्भायाः अधरः खण्डितः lit. bit the lower lip of रम्भा (कतिधा taken with both) रंभा is " the wife of नलकूबर and considered as the most beautiful woman in the paradise of India ". कतिधा because of the manifold births. " खण्डितो रतिरभसवशाच्चुम्बनावसरे कदाचिद्दन्तेनापि क्षत इति यावत. " भ्राम्यत् wandering in the world मधुरिम्णः उद्गार : the stream of sweetness.

14. कृष्णेति वर्णद्वयं विजयते । Here are series of metaphors and कृष्ण is poetically identified with so many things.

वज्रं पापमहीभृतां–पापानि एव महीभृत : i.e. mountains in the form of sins. तेषाम् वज्रम्–[Mythology:—The demon हिरण्याक्ष–by his magical powers endowed mountains with wings and they used to pound down the cities on which they would rest at their sweet will. God Indra, being touched by the feeling of humanity for the people of those cities clipped the wings of those mountains with his thunderbolt (वज्र) Hence the वज्र strikes terrors to mountains. (हरिवंश)] महीं बिभ्रति इति महीभृतः । भवः (संसारः) एव गदः (disease) तस्य उद्रेकः (excess) तस्य । 'रोगव्याधिगदामयाः' सिद्धं च तद् औषधं च । Specific medicine or antedote. मिथ्याज्ञानं-Erroneous Knowledge; it consists of considering the Supreme Being as different from the individual soul (जीवात्मा)

तिग्मा: अंशव: यस्य स: । तिग्मांशु: तस्य बिंबस्य उदय: one whose rays are hot i. e. The Sun. मिथ्याज्ञानं एव निशा तस्या यद् विशालं तम: तस्य । मह्यां रोहन्ति इति महीरुहः (trees) क्रूरा: क्लेशा: एव महीरुहः तेषाम् । उरुतरा: (gigantic) ज्वाला: ताभि: जटाल: (increased-encircled) " शिखावानाशुशुक्षणि: " शिखावान् means शिखी (शिखिन्) i. e. fire. निर्वृति: refers to the final beatitude निर्वृते: सद्म, तस्य (house of final: beatitude.)

15. चारयन् Pre. Pass. from the caus. of चर् grazing, feeding. गवां वृन्दं (1) the multitude of Kine (2) the group of senses (गो) नव: अम्बुद: तस्य निभा इव निभा यस्य असौ (श्रीकृष्ण:) like the new cloud-this refers to श्रीकृष्ण on account of his dark complexion. सौन्दर्यस्य अमृतं-nectar of his beauty. उद्गिरद्भि: Vomitting-giving out-emitting-संमोह्य gerund of the caus. of सं+मुह Having tempted or enticed. v.l. 'संयोज्य'-having joined to, it is not so happy. मन्दस्मितै:-by his slow smiles i. e. charming smiles. वल्लभ-dear. क्षयं नेष्यति-will lead to ruin.

The poet here resorts to the out—of—the way but at the same time the most telling poetic device in order to give vent to his devotion to श्रीकृष्ण.

By " बन्धु र्न कार्य: " he means " स एवबन्धु : कार्य: " because the reason which he asserts is that he will give you मोक्ष final beatitude and " a giver of मोक्ष " (मोक्षद:) is not to be neglected. Thus the poet intends to bring out the positive meaning by the emphatic negative expression.

16. अव्याख्येयां—Inexplicable-indescribable वितरति-प्रयच्छति-gives imparts. अन्तर्निमग्ना-when it occupies the interior of the heart. कण्ठे लग्ना-when it is attached to the

throat i.e. when it is repeated. आन्तरं ध्वान्तस्य जालम्-the mass of the internal darkness. This refers to the मिथ्याज्ञान of the अद्वैतवेदान्तिन्s some may construe this-as अन्तरस्य (अन्तः-करणस्य) ध्वान्तस्य (अज्ञान तमसः) जालं i.e. the mass of the darkness of the heart. द्राक्षा द्यैः by the grapes etc. द्राक्षाः आद्याः येषां ते-तैः । V.l. द्राक्षार्थैः=द्राक्षामौल्यैः (अर्थ means wealth and hence price) v.l. द्राक्षौघैः by the clusters of the grapes. द्राक्षाद्यैरपि बहुमतां. Highly regarded even by the grapes etc., i.e. superior to even the grapes in sweetness. आख्या—name. " रसज्ञा रसना जिह्वा " रसं जानाति इति रसज्ञा.

17. रम्यं रूपं येषां ते Having beautiful forms. अधिगताः अक्षं अक्षेण वा, अध्यक्षाः तैः-fallen in the range of sight (अक्षं= sense) v. l. उर्ध्वाक्षैः-ऊर्ध्वे अक्षिणी येषां ते तैः with their eyes raised up. अध्यक्षः-' प्रत्यक्षेऽधिकृतेऽध्यक्ष " निजस्यसखा-निजसखः-तम्-one's own friend " राजाहःसखिभ्यष्टच् " (Pan. 5-4-91.) नीरद नीरं जलं ददाति इति-that which gives water, a cloud. किमपि indescribable " कृष्ण " अभिधानं यस्य तत् whose name is 'कृष्ण' चित्तं आरूढं--चिन्तारूढं-rising to own mind.

18. विष्वद्रीच्या formed irregularly by विष्वग्देवयोश्च (Pan. 6-3-92) (original word विष्वद्र्यच-fem. from विष्वद्रीची) pervading everywhere.

विष्वद्द्युत्या विष्वग्समंततः and रुचिः lustre i. e. brightening all around. भासते etc. cf:—तमेव भान्तमनुभाति सर्वम् । तस्य भासा सर्वमिदं विभाति (मुं. 2-2-10) v. l. अहमिति प्रत्ययालंबनं अहंवृत्तिस्फुरणाश्रयः-the support of the consciousness of 'I'ness. or "अहं ब्रह्म " It is said "अहंवृत्तिरिदंवृतिरित्यन्तः करणं द्विधा । विज्ञानं स्यादहंवृत्तिर्मनोभवेत् । 'अहं' इति अहंकारः-Ego. v.l. स्वहृदयमतावेदिनः-स्वहृदयस्य मतं न विदन्ति not knowing the opinion of their own hearts. v. l. स्वहृदयतलावेदिनः Here, तलं=Real form. ०अनावेदिनः i. e. not knowing their own hearts. अन्यायोऽयं

शिव शिव ! Alas ! this is impropriety, the injustice referred to is fully expressed in the following couplet.

" योऽन्यथासन्तमात्मानमन्यथा प्रतिपद्यते ।
किं तेन न कृतं पापं चोरेणात्मापहारिणा " ॥

This verse brings in a nutshell the whole philosophy of the "Upnishads" in unambiguous expressions. The first line points out that the whole universe depends upon that Brahman for lustre i.e. life. The second line shows that the जीव has no existence apart from ब्रह्मन् and the third states that one's heart is the receptacle of ब्रह्मन् as expressed in " (एष मे आत्मा अन्तर्हृदये " Ch. 3–14 and " ईश्वर: सर्वभूतानां हृद्देशेऽर्जुन तिष्ठति " Bhagawat. G. 18–′1.

19. This is an advice of the poet to his mind. सेवा-service. चिन्ता means not "anxiety" as is generally taken but here it means " contemplating over. " चक्रम् आयुधं यस्य स: (बहु) i.e. Shri Vishnu. आलाप: means conversation. स्मरस्य रिपु: i.e. शङ्कर: v.l. स्मरगुरो: i.e. the father of Cupid (प्रद्युम्न) i.e. श्रीकृष्ण and therefore, this reading is better to suit this reading "गाथा" meaning " Bhagwat Gita." स्मररिपोर्गाथा i.e. verses dealing with शिव. स्वाप: sleep. निर्गता अर्गला (chain–limit) यस्मात् तत् adj. to सुखम् i.e. happiness, unlimited or unbounded. सुप्यताम् is the Imperative 3rd person sing. of the passive of स्वप् (2nd conj. p.) " to sleep."

20. "कलुषं वृजिनैनोऽघमंहो दुरितदुष्कृतम् " दूरिकृतंकलुषाणं जालं यै:(बहु) who have removed the bondage of sin " सुकृती पुण्यवान् धन्य: " भव: एव ग्रीष्म: तस्य प्रौढ: आतप: तस्य निवह: (mass) तेन संतप्तानि वपूंषि येषां ते i.e. whose bodies are heated by the mass of excessive heat of the summer in the form of this worldly existence. निगड=chain. अविवेकस्य व्यतिकर:

(आधिक्यं)–the contact of thoughtlessness (आत्मनात्मविवेकशून्यता) उन्मूल् 10 v. to uproot. आत्मा एव अमृतं तस्य सरः the lake of the nectar of Atma. नैराश्येनशि शिरं तस्मिन्–cool on account of hoplessness for as long as hopes are there none can enjoy the bliss of आत्मन् cf. आशा हि परमं दुःखं नैराश्यं परमं सुखम् । (Bhagwat. 11–8–44)

21. बन्धात् उन्मुक्तिः freedom from bondage (of this worldly existence) मखाः मुखे येषां ते adj. to कर्मपाशाः (पाश at the end of a compound expresses) "abundance, mass." Hence कर्मपाश–myriads of कर्मs "मखमुखाः कर्मपाशाः i. e. the myriads of कर्मs of which the sacrifice is the most important. मुनीनां शतानि तेषां मतानि तेषां अनल्पा (बहुधा) चिन्ता (चिन्तनं)–deep contemplation of the opinions of hundreds of sages All these sages claim that their opinion alone is the one which leads to final beatitude - for example the सांख्य of कपिल, वेदान्त of बादरायण, मीमांसा of जैमिनी and many others. अशुभानि एव जलधिः the sea of sins. मज्जन्ति bathe (मस्ज् 1 P.) तीर्थं a holy place of pilgrimage, a place of water. निपानागमयोस्तीर्थं ऋषिजुष्टजले गुरौ" भवे भ्रान्ति (perplexion) भजन्ते–who have missed their right way (getting ब्रह्मज्ञान) in this world. प्रामादिकं Erroneous.

Here जगन्नाथपण्डित condemns (1) the rites as being instrumental in bringing about freedom from bondange. cf. इष्टापूर्तं मन्यमानाः वरिष्ठं नान्यच्छ्रेयो वेदयन्ते प्रमूढाः Muri. 1–2–10

He next points out the inefficiency of the study of दर्शनs (Books on philosophy) as leading to tranquillity "नायमात्मा प्रवचनेन लभ्यो न मेधया न बहुना श्रुतेन" Muri.3–2–3.

Thirdly, he has no faith in the religious merits produced by pilgrimages for surmounting sins (cf. शुचिमनो यद्यस्ति तीर्थेन किम् । Bh. 2–55).

22. चुम्बितौ चरणौ यया सा resting on the feet; जंघे च (legs from ankle to the knee) जानू च (the two knees) ऊरू च (the thighs) नाभिः च हृदयं च=जङ्घा...हृदयानि आश्लिष्य embracing (i. e. contemplating over) मुखं अब्जं इव. It is customary to begin the contemplation over God from the leg, proceeding upwards to the head.

23. भूयात् is the benedictive third pers. of भू may I reside in the great soul (परमात्मा); this soul described as being free from all dualism (द्वैत) परमात्मनि स्थितिः that परमात्मा is not different from जीवात्मा one who has reached this stage does not differentiate between likes and dislikes cf:–दुःखेष्वनुद्विग्नमनाः सुखेषु विगतस्पृहः वीतरागभयक्रोधः– B. G. 2–56 निर्दोषं हि समं ब्रह्म (B. G. 5 19) निरन्तरा–निर्गतं अन्तरं यस्यां सा adj. to स्थितिः a condition of mental equipoise where one does not see any difference between himself and any other thing and between the things themselves. The great Shankaracharaya very aptly says.

"कल्यार्णव इवात्यन्त परिपूर्णैकवस्तुनि ।
निर्विकारे निराकारे निर्विशेषे भिदा कुतः । विवेक चूडामणि. 403

मलयानिलश्च कालकूटश्च तयोः between the breeze coming from the मलय mountain (which is very cool because it comes form sandal trees there on) and the deadly poison. रमण्याः कुन्तलाः the hair of a beautiful woman. भोगिनः भोगः the body of a serpent "अहेः शरीरंभोगः स्यात्" "उरगः पन्नगो भोगी जिह्मगः पवनाशनः" श्वानं पचति सः one who cooks a dog i e. the चण्डाल who is generally seen to be ugly. आत्मभूः one who is born of himself i.e. cupid "पुष्पधन्वा रतिपतिर्मकरध्वज आत्मभूः" who is the ideal of beauty in th world. . Such a condition of mind alone is capable of giving the ब्रह्मानन्द, the everlasting joy.

24. नश्वरं momentary–perishable; कलेवरं–शरीरं–Body. "अथ कलेवरं गात्रं वपुः संहननं शरीरं" तस्य कृते-for its sake. " कृते " "for" governs the genitive. कियान् how great ?

25. पले पले=प्रतिपलं At every moment. विरमति–रम् by itself is Atmanepadi but with वि becomes Parasmaipadi. See "व्याङ्परिभ्यो रमः" (Pan. 1–3–83) "वि+रम्" " to desist from " in the latter sense it governs the ablative cf. '**न निश्चितार्थाद् विरमन्ति** धीराः Bh. 2–80.

26. सपदि- at once. कृपाणस्य धाराः blades or edges of swords. अपहरतुतरां may much more take away. तराम्– Comparative termination is appended to verbal forms. cf. जयतितराम्, गच्छतितराम्. कृतान्तः–God of Death. " कृतान्तो यमुनाभ्राता शमनो यमराड् यमः" मनाग् a little.

27. This should be supposed to be the speech of one who deliberately restrains from talking anything that is offensive even to his enemy.

निरन्तरं incessantly; बहलः च असौ दहनः च तस्य जालम् a net of excessive fire. धमतु may blow. Imperative third pers. sing. from 'ध्मा' to blow. अप+भाष् to talk ill of.

28. This is the sum and substance of the poet's भक्ति–philosophy.

ताम्यसि–Pres. 2nd per. sing. of तम् 4. to pine, to be afflicted. तरणस्य उपायः–A remedy–means to cross (the sea of mortal existence.) The poet means that his जीव need not worry if it does not yet find any means, because only the remembrance of Lord Krishna at the time of death is sufficient to give it eternal freedom: Vide अन्तकाले च मामेव स्मरन्मुक्त्वा कलेवरम् । यः प्रयाति त्यजन्देहं स याति परमां गतिम् । (Bh. Gita 8–5)

चेतःसरणौ– चित्तवृत्तौ न आगन्ता 3rd pers. sing. of the first future of आ+गम्.

29. मद्यन्ती (full of rut) या गजघटा (a crowd of elephants) तस्याः मदः तस्मिन् भ्राम्यन्ती (hovering) या भृङ्गाणां आवलिः (row of bees) तस्याः मधुरः, झंकारः तेन सुभगाः adj. to श्रियः द्रविणं एव मदिरा तेन घूर्णिता (rolling) दृक् (sight) येषां–तेषाम्–with the eyesight rolling–unsteady–owing to the wine in the form of wealth. अय्=to go. सपर्या–worship. "पूजानमस्यापचितिः सपर्यार्चार्हणाः समाः" सौकर्य–facility. Very adequately; here the devotee prays that he should never grow rich lest he will forget the worship of his favourite deity. With this compare what कुन्ती says in the पाण्डवगीता–"विपदः सन्तु नः शश्वत् यासु संकीर्त्यते हरिः" ॥

30. This is an address of the poet to his own soul. वयसः शेषे–in the remnant of life, (since the poet is uttering this perhaps in old age.) निःशंकं–निर्गता शंका यथा स्यात् तथा (अव्ययी.) without any fear of the catastrophe (Death) impending upon him. जागर्ति–is awake. The poet has extreme faith in the unique purifying influence of the Ganges and he has composed a number of memorable verses called the–गङ्गालहरी in praise of the divine river. His utter faith in गङ्गा as his sure saviour is manifested in the following verse :–

> त्रपन्ते तीर्थानि त्वरितमिह यस्योद्धृतिविधौ
> करं कर्णे कुर्वन्त्यपि किल कपालिप्रभृतयः : ।
> इमं तं मामम्ब त्वमियमनुकम्पार्द्रहृदये
> पुनाना सर्वेषामघशमनदर्पं दलयसि ॥ गंगा० २८ ॥
> सुखं शेते मातस्तव खलु कृपातः पुनरयं
> जगन्नाथः शश्वत्त्वयि निहितलोकद्वयभरः ॥ गंगा० ३६ ॥

Hence he does not fear eventhough death overtakes him since the Ganga is sure to save him.

Tradition attributes to first-half of this verse to अप्पयदीक्षित, the author of कुवलयानन्द,-a work on rhetorics and a famous Pandit of the Dravida Country; and a contemporary of जगन्नाथ. Once when he visited Benares (वाराणसी), while returning home from the river Ganges, he chanced to see some person lying on the steps (घाट) leading to the river, embracing his young wife, and could be judged as old from his white hair on the head, which were visible, although all his body was covered with a garment; overcome by anger, astonishment and pity, simultaneously he exclaimed:—

"किं निःशंकं शेषे शेषे वयसि त्वमागते मृत्यौ" At this पण्डितराज raised his garment and saw the adviser. But seeing that the person was जगन्नाथ-himself lying there. अप्पय-दीक्षित added the second line अथवा...जननी because he was conversant with Jagannatha's immenes faith in the river and her reciprocal favour for जगन्नाथ.

31. धावं धावम्-णमुल् from धाव् to run, to struggle; धावं धावं i. e. running frequently-struggling after every thing in this world. v. l. सम्पादयामि यदयं for सन्तापयामि हृदयं. The reading does not seem to be so important.

32. मनसः भवः यस्य सः-मनोभवः (cupid-mind-born). तस्य शासनस्य (i. e. शिवस्य) पादौ एव अम्बुजे तयोः द्वयम् । अनारतं-Incessantly-संसृतिः (संसारः) एव गर्तः (pit) तस्य मध्ये । v. l. आमनन्तं-Thinking of or contemplating over, instead of आनमन्तम्.

Idea :-The poet means that his mind would not forget its grief for its child (Cupid) by throwing him (the poet) into the worldly existence as a punishment for his act of bowing to the feet of the burner of its son (Cupid).

Here the reference is to the incident of the burning of मदन by शंकर when the former undertook the work of bringing about the union of शंकर and पार्वती in order to beget a son to kill the demon तारक (see कुमार cantos 2 & 3).

33. मरकतमणीनां मेदिनीधरः–मेदिन्याः धरः–the mountain of emeralds. ऋषीणां निकरैः By the multitudes of sages. प्रपेदे Pass. Perf. 3rd pers. Sing. from प्र + पद्.

Idea:–Here various doubts arise in the minds of sages at the sight of Rama of dark blue complexion in in the " Dandaka forest." Of course these doubts are based on poetic comparison.

34. तरणेः (सूर्यस्य) तनया=यमुना, तोयमयी–full of water. मरकतमणिः (an emerald) तस्य ज्योत्स्ना its lustre. विलोकने तत्परैः engrossed or absorbed in seeing. उदितं कुतुकं येषु ते–तैः curious. कायस्य च्छाया–the complexion of the body. "कायोदेहः क्लीबपुंसोः " सन्दिदिहे is the pass. perf. of सम् + दिह् to be in doubt, to mistake for.

35. तरुषु मुख्यः the best of trees i. e. कल्पद्रुम मनीषिन्–Intelligent, wise " धीरो मनीषी ज्ञः प्राज्ञः " अथ here shows आनन्तर्य i.e. after he entertained so many misconceptions. गुरुभिः निश्वसितैः long deep sighs. वियोगोऽस्ति यस्याः सा वियोगिनी–one who is separated from her husband; निरणैषीत् Aorist 3rd per. sing of निर्+नी to ascertain.

36. दारिद्र्यस्य कोलाहलः–uproar of poverty. भूतिः–prosperity. असतः पथः जुषः–Resorting to an evil path. समा=year "हायनोऽस्त्री शरत्समाः" कोपः एव दहनः तस्य ज्वालाभिः जटालाः–filled with flames of the fire in the form of anger. जगतः ईशः–the ruler of the world

37. रत्नानि सानौ यस्य सः रत्नसानुः " मेरुः सुमेरुर्हेमाद्री रत्नसानुः सुरालयः" The mountain मेरु is the northern–most

mountain on the earth according to Indian mythology. आ is used सीमार्थे cf. सोऽहमाजन्मशुद्धानाम् Raghu 1-5. मलयेन वलयिताद्-encircled by the Malaya mountain (which is in the south and known as the Home of Sandals) कूलम्-shore "कूलं रोधश्च तीरं च"

पयांसि धीयन्ते यत्र इति पयोधि: i. e. the ocean. काव्यानां प्रणयने पटवः-well versed in composing poems. विगता शङ्का यस्मिन् कर्मणि तत्तया-निःशंकं i e. undoubtedly-without any doubt. मृद्वीकायाः मध्यः तस्माद् निर्यन्ती (coming out) या मसृणा (soft-delicate) रसस्य झरी (a stream-let) तस्याः माधुरी तस्य भाग्यं भजताम् (adj. to वाचाम्) v. l. काव्ये प्रणयनपटवः and v. l. ०झरीभाग्यभाजां नृपाणां-this reading is not very happy, we shall have to supply 'सभायां' after नृपाणां and ०भाजां becomes the adj. to नृपाणाम्.

Idea:—This poem and also the next two serve as a challenge of our poet in the art of writing poems. His are the most melodious poems and consequently he is the only blessed poet. Taking into consideration the worth of his poems, we can assert this much that his is not an empty boast. He has a remarkable command over Sanskrit Language. He means to say that sweetness of his poems surpasses that of even grapes as he has repeated elsewhere in this book.

38. गिरां देवी-Goddess of speech-the deity presiding over speech. गुण:-string-Here it refers to the string of the lute. रणनं-playing upon (वादनं) v. l. रसनं (tune or sound). हीनादर:-हीन: आदर: यस्य स: adj. to कर: i. e. having no regard for; and वीणाया: गुणानां रणने हीनादर: कर: यस्याः सा-whose hand lost (quitted) its fondness for playing upon the strings of a lute (वीणा) v. l. ०हीनादरकला-whose art is inferior-not so happy. यदीय like मदीय (mine) त्वदीय

(thine) अस्मदीय, युष्मदीय, तदीय–is an adjective and hence it qualifies वाचाम्. अमृतमयम्–full of nectar. श्रवणयो: सुभगं charming to ears. पण्डितानां पति:–तस्य–it refers to जगन्नाथराय himself who considers himself to be the lord of the poets. अधुन्वन् i. e. न धुन्वन् not nodding (his head) v. l. अमृतमथम्. for. मयम् अमृतं मथ्नाति इति–surpassing nectar. नृपशु: अथवा पशुपति: नृपशु: i. e. नृषु पशु: or ना पशुः इव or ना एव पशु: means the beast among men, or a beast in the form of a man. He means to say that the non-appreciator of his poem must be either a beast or he must be above every thing i. e. he must be a मुक्त like पशुपति i. e. entirely liberated from this transmigratory existence-he who has lost all charms for poems. पशुपति: i. e. God Shiva who is supposed to be a मुक्त (य: पुरस्ताद्यतीनाम् Malvika 1-1.)

सुभाषितेन गीतेन युवतीनां च लीलया ।
यस्य नो द्रवते चित्तं स वै मुक्तोऽथवा पशु: ॥

39. साक्षाद् अमृतम्–nectar incarnate i.e. nectar itself अथ and also cf. गणितमथ कलांकौशिकीम् " (Mk. 1.) वामानां (सुन्दरस्त्रीणां) अधरे या सुधा सा–nectar on the lower lips of lovely ladies. वामं सव्ये प्रतीपे च द्रविणे चातिसुन्दरे " इति विश्व:– विदधीरन्–Pot. Atm. 3rd per. plu. form of धा with वि. to do "3rd conj. V." मुद्–joy–अहह ! alas ! " अहहेत्यद्भुते खेदे परिक्लेशप्रकर्षयो: " cf.–अहह कष्टमपण्डितता विधे: (Bh. III-110) मन्दा मति: येषां ते–मन्दमतय: Dullards–the sluggish persons. जगन्नाथस्य भणिति: the words of Jagannath i.e. His poems.

40. This verse should be supposed to be a piece of advice given by जगन्नाथ to one of his brothers in profession. यदि (त्वं) अत्यन्तपाक द्रवन्मृद्वीकामधुमाधुरीमदपरीहारोध्दुराणां गिरां निर्माणे नितरां मार्मिकोऽसि, तर्हि, सखे, त्वं मादृशां संमुखे सुखेन काव्यं

कथय, नो चेत्, आत्मना कृतं दुष्कृतं इव (स्वकाव्यं) स्वान्ताद् बहिः मा (अ) कृथाः ।

अत्यन्तः पाकः (full ripening) तेन द्रवन् यद् मृद्वीकामधु (the juice dropping from grapes) तस्य माधुर्याः मदः (the pride of sweetness) तस्य परीहारे (removing) उद्धुराः adj. to गिरः. उद्धुर=Victorious–successful; मार्मिकः–capable–able. संमुखे-पुरतः, स्वान्ताद् बहिः–out of your own mind i.e. Don't show it to anybody lest it might be condemned. [मादृशां संमुखे shows the immense confidence of the poet in his own unique capacity as a poet and the perusal of his works leads us to think that he is quite justified in his self-eulogy. See also verse 34.

41. This poem is addressed by जगन्नाथ to his own "speech" which is disheartened because of the deliberate disrespect shown towards it by the wicked through jealousy.

हे मद्वाणि मात्सर्यमग्नमनसां खलानां अनादरेण विषादं मा कुरु । (यतः)
(त्वं काव्यारविंदमकरन्द मधुव्रतानां आस्येषु कियतो विलासान् धास्यसितमाम् ।

मात्सर्ये मग्नानि मनांसि येषां ते–तेषाम्–whose minds are full of jealousy; काव्यं एव अरविन्दं (lotus) तस्य मकरन्दस्य मधुव्रताः (bees) तेषाम्, आस्येषु (on the faces) कियतः विलासान् धास्यतितमाम् i.e. the satisfaction arising from the approbation of your poetry will be visible on the very faces of the readers of poetry. It points to a very general truth that a सहृदय alone can appreciate the beauty of a काव्य, none else, irrespective of his immense intelligence or erudition. cf.–बोद्धारो मत्सरग्रस्ताः प्रभवस्मयदूषिताः (Bh. N. 2).

42. परेषां वचसां श्लाघ्याः Praising the words (poems) of others. वाचंयमाः–Restraining their own speech; the idea is that learned men, although they appreciate and realize the worth of the poetry, written by others, will

be very cherry in expressing their admiration, through rivalry or jealousy. cf. प्राय: समानविद्या: परस्परयश:पुरोभागा: । Mal. Agni. 1-20. वाचं (नि) यच्छन्ति ते वाचंयमा:; कमलाया: (of Laxmi) विलासा: (sports) एव मदिरा तस्या: उन्मीलन् (produced) य: मद: (pride) तेन आघूर्णिता: (staggering, blinded). i. e. staggering or blinded by the intoxication (pride) of the wine in the form of sports of Laxmi; विपाक:—the exuberance (of my speech) i.e. my best poetry. कामेन अलसा: (impassioned)या: स्वर्वामा: (Heavenly damsels) cf. "वामा वनिता महिला तथा"—तासां अधरस्य माधुरी (the sweetness of the lower lip) तां अधरयन् i.e. exceeding the sweetness of the lower lip of the heavenly damsels. अधरयन् Pres. Part. from अधर (low) i.e. reducing them to a position of subsidiary importance. लास्यं—Dance (of pleasure).

43. धुर्य i. e. the best " धूर्वहे धुर्यधौरेय धुरीणास्तु धुरन्धरा: " इक्षु: sugarcane. माक्षिक–honey (मक्षिकाभि: कृतम्) v. l. माधुर्ये in sweetness; this reading is better and v. l. द्राक्षा...माक्षिकादीनाम् ।

44 आकलीतानि P. P. P. कल् with आ, were mastered-grasped-comprehended; नित्या: च ते विधय: च–usual duties (expected of a Brahman); संभाविता:–P. P. P. from the causal of भू with सम्; were attended to-were performed. दिल्लया: वल्लभस्यपाणिपाल्लवयो: पाणी एव पल्लवौ-कर्म.) तले i. e. under the kind patronage of the king of Delhi (lit. under the blossom-like hands of the king of Delhi) नवीनं वय: the prime of life or the flower of life i. e. youth. उज्झिता: वासना: यस्मिन् कर्मणि तद्यथास्यात्तथा—In a manner in which all the desires are given up. मधुपुरी refers to the City of Muttra-it was formerly the city of the demon मधु. v. l. संप्रत्यन्धकशासनस्य नगरे तत्त्वं परं चिन्त्यते । (the punisher of the Demon) अन्धक–vide मत्स्यपुराण 178. तस्य नगरम्=Benares.

पण्डितराजानां राजिषु तिलकः—the foremost of the lines of princes of poets. अकारि–Pass. Aorist 3rd per. sing form कृ 8 U. to do–was done. लोकाधिकम्–more than (other) people.

45. जारेभ्य. जन्मानि येषां ते–Born of paramours. शङ्का-fear; पद्यानि एव रत्नानि-तेषां मञ्जुषा i. e. a box " पिटकः पेटकः पेटा मञ्जुषा " Jagannath in this concluding verse gives the reason why he has locked up all his verses in this book called भामिनीविलास. He says that he has done so to guard himself against plagiarists (literary thieves). All the verses contained in the present book are scattered severally in his other works like the रसगङ्गाधर and hence, his apprehension of the fear.

APPENDIX A.

१ प्रास्ताविकविलासः

दृढप्रेमा भग्नः सदसिरिव संधिं न लभते
लमेताभिप्रायः स्खलति बहुयत्नैरपि धृतः ।
स्खलेन्नो चेत्साम्यं न भजति भजेद्वा न पवति
च्युतं संगच्छेत स्मृतिमुपगतस्तु व्यथयति ॥ १ ॥

This is what is given in Mr. Vaidya's edition. Herein some words are difficult to be construed and are perhaps misread and miswritten. As given in the सुभाषितरत्नभाण्डागार the verse runs thus—

दृढप्रेमा भग्नः सदसिरिव संधिं न भजते
भजेतापि प्रायः स्खलति खलु यत्नैरपि धृतः ।
स्खलेन्नो चेत् साम्यं भजति न, भजेद्वा न भवति
च्युताशङ्कश्चेत्स्यात् स्मृतिमुपगतस्तु व्यथयति ॥ १ ॥

This verse describes how friendship once broken cannot be revived and made as strong or efficient as it originally was.

दृढः प्रेमा (यदि) भग्नः (चेत्) सदसिः इव संधिं न भजते, (संधिं) भजेत अपि यत्नैः अपि खलु धृतः प्रायः स्खलति, नो स्खलेत् चेत् (पूर्वप्रेम्णा) साम्यं न भजति; (साम्यं) भजेद्वा न (पूर्ववद्) भवति; च्युताशङ्कः चेत् स्यात् तु स्मृतिमुपगतः व्यथयति ।

दृढः sincere, everlasting. प्रेमन् (m) love. सद् + असिः a good sword. संधिं न लभते cannot be joined. स्खलति breaks. साम्यं न भजति–does not reach the original standard. न भवति does not last long, does not grow powerful. च्युता आशंका यस्मिन् सः adj. to प्रेमा where the distrust or apprehension due to the breach of friendship has disappeared because of the compromise that is brought about between two friends. तु–yet, even when the compromise is effected. व्यथयति–produces pain–rankles in the heart. i. e. the effect of the breach of friendship persists even then. The simile with असि may be sustained further, where applicable.

The staunch friendship when broken is not joined like a good sword even though it is joined, it becomes loose although it is maintained by endeavours, if it does not get loose, it does not approach the original sincerity, or if it is reached, it does not last for a long time, if the doubt disappears, the remembrance of the lost friendship rankles in the heart.

(२)

कातराः परदुःखेषु निजदुःखेष्वकातराः
अर्थेष्वलोभा, यशसि सलोभाः, संति साधवः ॥ २ ॥

कातराः grieved. नास्ति लोभः येषु ते–not covetous.

Good men feel distressed at the griefs of others, and are not distressed at their own griefs. They are not covetous of money but they covet fame.

(३)

विद्वत्सु विमलज्ञाना विरक्ता यतिषु स्थिताः
स्वीयेषु तु गरोद्गाराः नराकाराः क्षितौ खलाः ॥ ३ ॥

क्षितौ नराकाराः खलाः विद्वत्सु विमलज्ञानाः (स्थिताः) यतिषु विरक्ताः स्वीयेषु तु गरोद्गाराः (स्थिताः)

नरस्य इव आकारः येषां ते–Having the form of human beings. विमलं ज्ञानं येषां ते. गरं इव उद्गाराः येषां ते whose words are like poison.

On this earth, wicked persons, disguised as men, show themselves as possessed of pure knowledge when they have to talk with learned persons, show themselves as free from all bondage, when they have to talk with Yatis, but when with their kinsmen, they eject venom in the form of their speech.

Additional verse in शांतविलास.

सुरस्रोतस्विन्या: पुलिनमधितिष्ठन्नयनयो:
विधायान्तर्मुद्रामथ सपदि विद्राव्य विषयान् ।
विधूतांतर्ध्वान्तो मधुरमधुरायां चिति कदा
निमग्न: स्यां कस्यांचन नवनभस्यांबुदरुचि ॥ १ ॥

सुरस्रोतस्विन्या: पुलिनमधितिष्ठन्, नयनयो: अंत: मुद्रां विधाय, अथ सपदि विषयान्विद्राव्य, विधूतान्तर्ध्वान्त: (अहं) कस्यांचन नवनभस्यांबुदरुचि मधुरमधुरायां चिति कदा निमग्न: स्याम् ।

सुराणां स्रोतस्विनी The river of gods i. e. the Ganges. पुलिनमधितिष्ठन् standing on the sandy bank. the acc. of पुलिन is according to अधिशीङ्स्थासां कर्म (Pan. 1–4–46) मुद्रां विधाय–Shutting or closing–closing the eyes inwards. The highest principle according to the Vedanta philosophy is visible only to those who look inwards, closing all communication with the outer world. This process of looking inwards with the object of getting परमात्मज्ञान has been referred to Katha. 2–1 in the mantra· परांचि खानि व्यतृणत् स्वयंभू: तस्मात्पराङ् पश्यति नान्तरात्मन् । कश्चिद् धीर: प्रत्यगात्मानमैक्षदावृत्तचक्षुरमृतत्वमिच्छन् ॥ विषयान् विद्राव्य is the gerund of the causal of वि + द्रु lit. causing the objects of senses to dissolve. i. e. when all the objects of sense are extinct or विषय may mean शब्द–स्पर्श etc. as in B. G. 18–51. शब्दादीन् विषयांस्त्यक्त्वा...ब्रह्मभूयाय कल्पते ॥ Because as long as these विषयs are intact, the bondage persists. विधूतं अन्त: (वर्तमानं) ध्वान्तं येन स: who has shaken off the internal ignorance. चित् knowledge, one of famous Trinity सत्–चित्–आनंद existence, knowledge and bliss.

The highest truth is often described as चित् cf. दिक्कालाद्यनवच्छिन्नानन्त**चिन्मात्रमूर्तये** । स्वानुभूत्येकमानाय नमः शान्ताय तेजसे ॥ (भर्तृ० ।–।) नवः नभस्ये (भाद्रपदे) अंबुदः तस्य रुग् (शोभा) इव रुग् यस्य–तस्मिन्–whose lustre–complexion–is like the new cloud in the month of भाद्रपद i. e. bluish. 'स्युर्नभस्यः प्रौष्ठपदभाद्भाद्रपदाः समाः' मधुरमधुरा very sweet.

When shall I be merged in the extremely sweet knowledge (i.e. कृष्ण) whose complexion–lustre–resembles that of a new cloud in the month of भाद्रपद, I–with the internal ignorance completely shaken off, am standing on the bank of the celestial river, after closing my eyes inward, immediately dissolving the objects of sense.

Appendix B.

APPENDIX C.

Metres occurring in the texts, with their definitions and schemes.

A stanza (पद्य) in Sanskrit Poetry is a combination of four quarters (पादs). A पाद is a combination of a certain number of syllables (अक्षरs) or of syllabic instants (मात्राs). A पद्य is either a वृत्त or जाति. A वृत्त is a stanza, the metre of which is regulated by the number and position of syllables in each quarter. A जाति is a stanza, the metre of which is regulated by the number of syllabic instants (मात्राs) in each quarter.

वृत्त

1 समवृत्त — 2 अर्धसमवृत्त — 3 विषमवृत्त

1 समवृत्त is a stanza in which the पादs composing the stanza are all similar.

2 अर्धसमवृत्त is a stanza in which the alternate quarters are similar.

3 विषमवृत्त is a stanza in which the quarters are all dissimilar.

Sanskrit poems are generally written in the वृत्त metres and only occasionally in the जाति, of which only the आर्या variety is most commonly used.

A syllable (अक्षर) is so much of a word as can be pronounced at once, i.e. a vowel with or without one or more consonants.

अक्षर

लघु (short) गुरु (long)

A syllabic instant (मात्रा) is the measure of time required to pronounce a short vowel.

A syllable ending in a short vowel is called लघु e.g. अ, इ, उ, ऋ, ऌ

A syllable ending in a long vowel, or one, though ending in a short vowel, yet followed by a conjunct consonant or an अनुस्वार or a विसर्ग, is called गुरु. "सानुस्वारश्च दीर्घश्च विसर्गी च गुरुर्भवेत्। वर्णः संयोगपूर्वश्च तथा पादान्तगोऽपि वा॥" छन्दोमञ्जरी.

The last syllable of a quarter (पाद) may be लघु or गुरु according as the metre requires it.

In metres regulated by the number of syllabic instants (मात्रा), a लघु vowel has one मात्रा and a गुरु one has two मात्राs.

For the purpose of scanning metres regulated by the number of syllables, each quarter (पाद) is divided into groups of three letters each. Each such group forms a syllabic foot and is styled as a गण. There are eight गणs, each being distinguished by the position of particular syllables, short or long, which it contains viz. य, र, त, भ, ज, स, म and न " आदिमध्यावसानेषु यरता यान्ति लाघवम्। भजसा गौरवं यान्ति मनौ तु गुरुलाघवम्.

The sign for ल (लघु) is ⏑ and for ग (गुरु) —

य ⏑ — —; र — ⏑ —; त — — ⏑; न ⏑ ⏑ ⏑.

भ — ⏑ ⏑; ज ⏑ — ⏑; स ⏑ ⏑ —; म — — —.

The following is the distribution of verses according to metres.

Name of Vritta.	No. of verses in Vilasa I.	No. in Vilsa IV
1 आर्या	1,7,10,13,21,22, 24,26,28,29,50,81, 90,92,97,98,102, 108,	25,31,43
2 शिखरिणी	2,32.33,40,43,52, 54,60,79,83,84	5 7,20,29,38,39, App. 4
3 पृथ्वी	3	1,2,3,4
4 शार्दूलविक्रीडितम्	4,16,31,34,35,38, 41,46,48,55,56,57, 58,59,63,66,67,72, 77,86,103,128.	10,11,13,14,15, 19,36,37,40,42, 44
5 मालिनी	5,36,121	
6 पुष्पिताग्रा	8,74	26,33
7 प्रहर्षिणीयम्	15,96,124	
8 वसंततिलका	17,37,47,49,69,70, 71,75,94.95,101, 104,105,122	8,32,41
9 मन्दाक्रान्ता	30	16,17,18,21
10 अनुष्टुभ्	39,62,65,78,87,88, 89,91,93,99,109, 110,112 115,116, 117,118,119,120, 126,127,129	9,45 App. 2,3
11 वैतालीय or वियोगिनी	44,111	35,23,24
12 उपेन्द्रवज्रा	45,125	
13 रथोद्धता	51	
14 गीति	12,6,9,14,18,20, 25,27 42,68,80, 100,106,114,123	22,27,28
15 मंजुभाषिणी	53	
16 उपगीति	61,64,73,82	
17 उद्गाति	11,19,76	12

18 उपजाति	73,85	
19 प्रमिताक्षरा	107	
20 द्रुतविलम्बितम्	113	
21 स्वागता		6
22 हरिणी		34

Characteristics of the metres given above.

1 **आर्या**—12 मात्राs in the 1st and 3rd पाद, 18 मात्राs in the second पाद and 15 in the fourth.
(This is the general characteristic)

2 **शिखरिणी**—रसै रुद्रैश्छिन्ना यमनसभलाग: शिखरिणी।
य, म, न, स, भ, and one short and one long letter with stops at 6 and 11.

3 **पृथ्वी**—जसौ जसयला वसुग्रहयतिश्च पृथ्वी गुरु:
ज, स, ज, स, य, one short and one long letter with stops at 8, 9.

4 **शार्दूलविक्रीडितम्**—सूर्याश्वैर्यदि म:सजौ सततगा: शार्दूलविक्रीडितम्।
म, स, ज, स, त, त, and one long letter with stops at 12, 7.

5 **मालिनी**—ननमयययुतेयं मालिनी भोगिलोकै:।
न, न, म, य, य with stops at 8, 7

6 **पुष्पिताग्रा**--अयुजि नयुगरेफतो यकारो
युजि तु नजौ जरगाश्च पुष्पिताग्रा।
न, न, र and य in odd quarters and न, ज, ज, र and ग in even quarters.

7 **प्रहर्षिणीयम्**—त्र्याशभिर्मनजरगा: प्रहर्षिणीयम्।
म, न, ज, र and one long letter with stops at 3, 10

8 **वसंततिलका**—उक्ता वसंततिलका तभजाजगौगा:।
त, भ, ज, ज, and two long letters.

9 **मन्दाक्रान्ता**--मन्दाक्रान्तांबुधिरसनगैर्मो भनौ तौ गयुग्मम्।
म, भ, न, त, त, and two long letters.

10 अनुष्टुभ्—श्लोके षष्ठं गुरु ज्ञेयं सर्वत्र लघु पंचमम् ।
द्विचतु:पादयोह्रस्वं सप्तमं, दीर्घमन्ययो: ।

11 वैतालीय—

12 उपेन्द्रवज्रा—ज, त, ज, and two long letters.
(same as इंद्रवज्रा with the exception of the first letter, which is short here).

13 रथोद्धता—रात्परैर्नरलगै रथोद्धता
र, न, र, and one short and one long letter.

14 गीति--12 syllabic instants in I and III quarter and 18 in II and IV.

15 मंजुभाषिणी—सजसा जगौ च यदि मंजुभाषिणी ।
स. ज, स, ज and one long letter.

16 उपगीति—12 syllabic instants in I and III quarter and 15 in II and IV.

17 उद्गीति—12 syllabic instants in I and III 15 in II and 18 in IV

18 उपजाति—mixture of इंद्रवज्रा and उपेंद्रवज्रा both of which have been given above.

19 प्रमिताक्षरा—सजससै: कथिता प्रमिताक्षरा
स, ज, स and स

20 द्रुतविलम्बितम्—द्रुतविलम्बितमाह नभौ भरौ ।
न, भ, भ and र

21 स्वागता—स्वागता रनभगैर्गुरुणा च ।
र, न, भ, and two long letters.

22 हरिणी—नसमरसला ग: षड्वेदैर्हयैर्हरिणीमता ।
न, स, म, र, स, one short and one long letter; stops at 6, 4, 7.

———